Thai
PHRASE
BOOK

Sanya Bunnag

Consultant:

Rachel Harrison

BBC Books

Contents

How to use this book

▌ Communicating in a foreign language doesn't have to be difficult – you can convey a lot with just a few words (plus a few gestures and a bit of mime). Just remember: keep it simple.

▌ The book is divided into sections for different situations. In each section you'll find:

▌ Useful tips and information

▌ Words and phrases that you'll see on signs and in print

▌ Phrases you are likely to want to say

▌ Things that people may say to you

▌ As Thai script is a totally different one to Roman alphabets, the authors have kept the Thai script to a minimum. Also, there are a few sounds in Thai that are different from anything you will ever come across in European languages. We strongly recommend you to start by taking a good look at the pronunciation guide and the guidance on how the Thai language works before you attempt to say any phrase in this book. The (Essential) Pronunciation Guide and the Basic Thai Grammar sections are on page 9 and 14 respectively.

▌ We also recommend you 'understand' some Thai culture before you visit the country because it is easy for people from western culture to unintentionally cause offence to people in eastern culture as in Thailand. The Culture section is on page 20.

▌ We have extensively listed many useful words in their own sections, for example, 'Parts of the body' and 'Diseases and medical problems' in the Health section; 'Shops' and 'Colours' in the Shopping section; and 'Basic condiments' in the Menu Reader section. So, if you can't find the words you want in the English-Thai dictionary which begins on page 136, please look them up in the relevant sections instead.

▌ You may find the Menu Reader section different from some other phrase books in that it has listed each dish in English before the Thai equivalent. The authors have come to the conclusion that unless one knows the Thai alphabets, it will be difficult for an average tourist to find what really is on the menu. So the idea is for you to study the menu reader before deciding what kinds of dishes you want to have and then look for the restaurant or food stall which offers them. Strictly speaking, it may not be a "menu reader" as such, but the authors guarantee that you will enjoy Thai cuisine much, much more.

▌ Wherever possible, work out in advance what you want to say – if you're going shopping, for instance, write out a shopping list in Thai. If you're buying travel tickets, work out how to say where you want to go, how many tickets you want, single or return, etc.

▌ Practise saying things out loud – the cassette that goes with this book will help you to get used to the sounds of Thai.

▌ Above all – don't be shy! Please remember that you don't need to pronounce everything perfectly. It'll be appreciated if you try to say a few words. Thais will usually try to help you when they see that you are trying to speak their language.

▌ The authors would welcome any suggestions or comments about this book, but in the meantime, have a good trip and enjoy your stay in Thailand – **tîaw hâi sa-nùk ná**.

The Thai alphabet

❚ Thai is one of the oldest languages in South-East Asia, but the Thai script has developed comparatively recently. It is of Sanskrit origin and was introduced by King Ramkamhaeng of Sukhothai Kingdom in the thirteenth century.

❚ Thai script, which is totally different from the Roman alphabet, consists of 44 consonants and 48 vowels. Written Thai runs from left to right but vowel signs, depending on the sign itself, may be written before, above, below and after consonants.

❚ Two of the consonants are now obsolete; this phrasebook will show the remaining 42 consonants as a guideline only. The vowel signs are not displayed.

❚ See the "Basic Thai Grammar" and "The Pronunciation Guide" sections for more details.

Thai Consonants:

ก   given the Thai name as   **gor** gài (as in 'a' for apple)

ข   given the Thai name as   **kŏr** kài

ค   given the Thai name as   **kor** kwai

ฆ   given the Thai name as   **kor** rá-kang

ง   given the Thai name as   **ngor** ngoo

จ   given the Thai name as   **jor** jarn

ฉ   given the Thai name as   **chŏr** chìng

ช   given the Thai name as   **chor** chárng

ซ   given the Thai name as   **sor** sôh

ฌ   given the Thai name as   **chor** ga-cher

ญ   given the Thai name as   **yor** yǐng

ฎ   given the Thai name as   **dor** chá-dar

ฏ   given the Thai name as   **Tor** Pa-Tàk

ฎ	given the Thai name as	**tŏr** săn-tărn
ฑ	given the Thai name as	**tor** narng-mon-toh
ฒ	given the Thai name as	**tor** pôo-tâo
ณ	given the Thai name as	**nor** nayn
ด	given the Thai name as	**dor** dèhk
ต	given the Thai name as	**Tor** Tào
ถ	given the Thai name as	**tŏr** tǔng
ท	given the Thai name as	**tor** ta-hǎrn
ธ	given the Thai name as	**tor** tong
น	given the Thai name as	**nor** nǒo
บ	given the Thai name as	**bor** bai-mái
ป	given the Thai name as	**Por** Plar
ผ	given the Thai name as	**pŏr** pêuhng
ฝ	given the Thai name as	**fŏr** făr
พ	given the Thai name as	**por** parn
ฟ	given the Thai name as	**for** fan
ภ	given the Thai name as	**por** săm-pao
ม	given the Thai name as	**mor** már
ย	given the Thai name as	**yor** yák
ร	given the Thai name as	**ror** reuar
ล	given the Thai name as	**lor** ling
ว	given the Thai name as	**wor** wăirn
ศ	given the Thai name as	**sŏr** săr-lar
ษ	given the Thai name as	**sŏr** reur-sěe
ส	given the Thai name as	**sŏr** sěuar
ห	given the Thai name as	**hŏr** hèep
ฬ	given the Thai name as	**lor** jù-lar
อ	given the Thai name as	**or** àrng
ฮ	given the Thai name as	**hor** nók-hôok

The (essential) pronunciation guide

▌ There are a few sounds in Thai that are totally different from anything you will ever come across in European languages. We have tried to represent these as simply as we can in the pronunciation system. Nevertheless, because Thai has so many different consonants and vowels, there is no way to write these in English without producing some pretty strange-looking combinations of letters! It's absolutely essential therefore that you start by taking a careful look at this pronunciation guide so that you can have a good crack at pronouncing Thai clearly.

Consonants

Thai consonant sounds are, for the most part, straightforward and have identifiable English equivalents. For example, some really easy ones are:

y – pronounced 'yuh', as in 'yes'

n – pronounced 'nuh', as in 'never'

r – pronounced 'ruh', as in 'red' (although most Thais pronounce 'r' as 'l')

l – pronounced 'luh', as in 'love'

w – pronounced 'wuh', as in 'walk'

The other Thai consonant sounds can be divided into two pronunciation groups – one of *aspirated* sounds, the other of *unaspirated* sounds. In case that all seems a bit complicated, we'll show you what we mean overleaf:

Aspirated sounds

k – pronounced as in 'king'

t – pronounced as in 'take'

s – pronounced as in 'sit'

p – pronounced as in 'pig'

b – pronounced as in 'bell'

d – pronounced as in 'dog'

f – pronounced as in 'fan'

h – pronounced as in 'happy'

ch – pronounced as in 'chase'

Unaspirated sounds

j – pronounced as in 'jelly'

Try, if you can, to make this 'j' sound slightly harder and more explosive than it does in English.

g – always pronounced as in 'get'

T – pronounced like 't' in English, with the aspiration removed

P – pronounced like 'p' in English, with the aspiration removed

Since we don't have either of these sounds in English, you will probably find them the most difficult to pronounce. Don't despair if you can't do it: it's not the end of the world if they sound like an ordinary, aspirated 'p' and 't'.

(Note that the unaspirated 't' and 'p' are represented by 'T' and 'P' in this phrasebook)

Another difficult consonant in Thai is :

ng – pronounced as in 'sing'

Although it is easy for us to say 'ng' when it is at the end of a word in English, we never have it at the beginning, as it can be in Thai.

When it comes at the start of a word, we tend to end up saying 'nug' or 'ugn' because we are so used to having a vowel in there. One way to practise saying 'ng' at the start of a word is by starting off saying sing and then taking off the 's' so you are left with 'ing'. That's still easy in English. It's taking off the 'i' so you are left with 'ng' that is the difficult part. Try doing this a few times and then have a go with other words like 'pang', 'lung' and 'gong'.

Vowels

As we mentioned before, there are many Thai vowels (48 altogether) to get your tongue around, and some of them produce very unusual sounds to the non-Thai's ear. One way of making the vowels seem less numerous is to think of them in pairs, with a short and a long version of each sound. For example:

a/ar, *i/ee*, *u/oo*, *aih/air*, *euh/eur* and *eh/ay*.

Other vowel sounds are made by combining two short vowels. For example:

'i' and 'a',	combined to make	'ia'
'u' and 'a',	combined to make	'ua'
'eur' and 'ar',	combined to make	'euar'

Vowel Sounds

a   pronounced as 'a' in 'pat'

ar   pronounced as 'ar' in 'ja'r

i   pronounced as 'i' in 'tin'

ee   pronounced as 'ee' in 'free'

air pronounced as 'air' in 'pair'

aih a shorter version of 'air'

u   pronounced as 'u' in 'put'

11

oo	pronounced as 'oo' in 'cool'
o	pronounced as 'o' in 'dot'
oh	pronounced as 'oh' in 'Oh dear!'
eh	pronounced as the short 'e' in 'pen'
ay	pronounced as 'ay' in 'pay'
oei	pronounced like the French word 'oeil' in 'trompe l'oeil'
er	pronounced as 'er' in 'germ'
euh	as we would say 'uh' in 'Uh? What's that? I didn't hear'
eur	a longer version of 'euh'
euar	a combination of 'eur' and 'a'
ua	pronounced as 'ure' in 'mature'
ia	pronounced as 'ea' in 'spear'
or	pronounced as 'or' in 'torn'
oy	pronounced as 'oy' in 'boy'
ai	pronounced like the 'y' in 'my' or the words 'I' or 'eye'
ao	pronounced like the 'ow' in 'now'

Tones

One thing that often worries people when they are trying to speak Thai is the fact that it's a tonal language. This means that every word or syllable has one of five tones, and it is important to try and put the tone in when you say a word, otherwise it could mean something else. Getting the tone of a word right is as important as being able to pronounce the consonants and vowels clearly. Although the example below is an extreme case, it does illustrate the point:

mǎi mài mâi mái means 'Does new silk burn?' and

mǎi mài mâi mâi means 'New silk does not burn'.

Another good example of this is the syllable **kar**. Said with a mid tone, it means 'to dangle', with a low tone it means **galanga** (a spice used in soups and curries), with a high tone it means 'to trade', with a falling tone 'to kill' and with a rising tone 'a leg'!

As you can see, Thai has five different tones. The easiest ones are probably the rising and the falling tones, since we do have something approximating to these in English intonation. When we assert something, for example, we tend to use a 'falling' intonation; and when we question something we use a 'rising' or querying intonation. This produces basically the same sound as the rising and falling tones in Thai, except that they are accentuated far more. In the phrasebook, we have indicated the rising tone with a ' ˇ ' mark and falling tone with a ' ^ '.

Perhaps surprisingly, one of the most difficult tones is the 'mid tone' because we rarely use a monotone in English, although we can if we remember. The 'low tone' is a variation on this – it's a monotone, but held at a lower pitch than the mid tone. Lastly, there's the 'high tone' which is definitely the hardest. It's a high-pitched tone, said as though you were squeezing out the sound, or having your neck wrung!

To represent the low tone, we have used a ' ` ' and the high tone is indicated by a ' ´ '. Where there is no mark at all over the syllable, this means it is pronounced with a mid tone.

Just to recap :

| ' ` ' | = | low tone | ' ^ ' | = | falling tone |
| ' ´ ' | = | high tone | ' ˇ ' | = | rising tone |

Basic Thai grammar

▌ One of the easier aspects of Thai, compared to most European languages, is its lack of complex grammar rules. You have no need to worry about changing verb endings or putting nouns into different cases. In fact, Thai lacks the strict definitions of word class (or parts of speech) that are essential to European languages, and the whole way of putting a sentence together can be very different. Expressing ideas in the past and the future tenses, for example, is extremely simple.

▌ There are no punctuation marks in Thai. For this reason, while you will see full stops, commas and question marks in the English phrases, you will not see them in the Thai versions.

▌ You must always remember that Thai has a very different structure from many European languages, so you should not aim to construct sentences in Thai in the same way as in English. It will not be possible, therefore, for you to find a word-for-word correlation between the English phrase and the Thai transliteration in this book.

Tenses

The past tense

If you are talking in Thai about something that has already happened, it is usually obvious from the context and there is no need to add a verbal past tense marker. If a sentence begins, for example, with the words **mêuar warn née** (yesterday), the word **láirw** (already) or the phrase **sŏrng Pee gòrn** (two years ago), all verbs are automatically *understood* to be in the past tense. In less clear cases, the word **láirw** can be attached to the end of the sentence. To illustrate this, take a look at the following sentences containing the words **káo** (he/she/they), **Pai** (to go) and **tam-ngarn** (to work):

káo Pai tam-ngarn	He **goes** to work
mêuar warn née káo Pai tam-ngarn	Yesterday he **went** to work
káo Pai tam-ngarn láirw	He **has gone** to work

The same thing happens in a sentence made with words like *gin* (to eat) and *kâo* (rice):

káo gin kâo	She **eats** rice
mêuar warn née káo gin kâo	Yesterday she **ate** rice
káo gin kâo láirw	She **has eaten** rice

The present continuous tense

In Thai, the way of showing that an action is in the process of taking place and has not yet been completed is to put the word **gam-lang** just in front of the main verb. For example:

káo gam-lang tam-ngarn	He **is working**
káo gam-lang dèurm nárm	She **is drinking** the water

The future tense

To make the future tense, you simply put **jà** directly in front of the main verb. For example:

káo jà tam-ngarn	He **will** work
káo jà dèurm nárm	She **will** drink the water

The verb 'to be' and adjectives

The verb 'to be' in Thai is *'Pehn'*, except when you want to say 'to be' in the sense of 'to be located', when the word *'yòo'* is used.

A couple of examples, using the words *káo* (he/she/they), *mŏr* (doctor), *rohng-rairm* (hotel), *têe* (in/at) and *grung-tâyp* (Bangkok), might help to make this clearer:

káo Pehn mŏr	He **is** a doctor
rohng-rairm yòo têe grung-tâyp	The hotel **is (located)** in Bangkok
káo Pehn mŏr yòo têe grung-tâyp	He is a doctor in Bangkok

There are times, however, when neither *Pehn* nor *yòo* are needed in Thai, but where we still use the verb 'to be' in English. This is when we use a subject and adjective in Thai, rather than a subject and a noun. The subject can be either an animate or an inanimate object. So while we *do* say *káo Pehn mŏr* (he is a doctor), the *Pehn* is dropped when we say something like 'he is fat' or 'he is good at his job'. These two sentences in Thai are simply *káo ûan* and *káo gèhng*, with no verb at all.

English differs from some European languages in that adjectives come before the noun unless used predicatively. In English, we say things like 'the fat doctor' or 'the clever woman'. In Thai, the order is reversd, i.e. adjectives come after the noun, so a phrase like *mŏr ûan* can either be a complete sentence, meaning 'the doctor is fat', or the subject of a longer sentence 'the fat doctor ...'

Here are a few examples of nouns and adjectives together, without, the verb *Pehn* (to be):

pôo-yǐng gèhng	A clever woman/Women are clever
rohng-rairm yài	A big hotel/The hotel is big
Prai-sa-nee glâi	A nearby post office/The post office is nearby
gar-fair yehn	Cold coffee/The coffee is cold
Pra-tâyt rórn	A hot country/The country is hot

Plural nouns and counting

You might have noticed from the first example above, *pôo-yǐng gěhng*, that it can mean 'women' as well as 'woman'. There is no special way of showing plurals in Thai; it is just another one of those things that are understood in context. So, a phrase like *rohng-rairm yài* can mean 'The hotel is big', referring to a specific hotel, or 'Hotels are big' in general.

Counting nouns in Thai is a rather more complicated business and certainly more elaborate than in English. To count anything in Thai requires not only the item being counted and the number, but also an extra word known as a *classifier* or word to measure it by. Every noun has its own classifier, and in most cases the choice of classifier is an obvious one. For example, portions of fried rice are measured or classified by the word plate (*jarn*), beer by the word glass (*gâirw*) or bottle (*kùat*), and cake by the word piece (*chín*).

For all measurements, the word order is as follows:

noun + number + classifier.

So we get:

káyk + *nèuhng* + *chín* / cake + one + piece = one piece of cake

kâo pàt + *sǒrng* + *jarn* / fried rice + two + plates = two plates of fried rice

bia + *sǎrm* + *kùat* / beer + three + bottles = three bottles of beer

nárm + *sèe* + *gâirw* / water + four + glasses = four glasses of water

Here's a list of some other classifiers that you might find useful:

kon	for people
Tua	for animals, tables, chairs and items of clothing
lôok	for fruit
bai	for fruit, paper and banknotes
forng	for eggs

17

cha-bàp   for letters and newspapers

lêhm   for books

Asking and answering questions

Answering questions in Thai is easy because all you need to do is follow exactly the same word order as the question, taking off the very last word and replacing it with the answer. Question words almost always come at the very end of the sentence and the most common ones are *mái* and *châi mái*.

There is no one word for 'yes' or 'no' in Thai, but for questions ending in *châi mái* the answer is *châi* if you wish to agree and *mâi châi* to disagree. Here are a few examples:

rohng-rairm yài châi mái	The hotel is big, isn't it?
châi	Yes
mâi châi	No
Prai-sa-nee glâi châi mái	The post office is near, isn't it?
châi	Yes
mâi châi	No
mŏr gèhng châi mái	The doctor is good, isn't he?
châi	Yes
mâi châi	No

Questions ending in *mái* are a bit more complicated to answer because you need to repeat the verb or the adjective. Look at the examples below to see how this is done.

rohng-rairm yài mái	Is the hotel big?
yài	Yes (literally: big)
mâi yài	No (literally: not big)
Prai-sa-nee glâi mái	Is the post office near?
glâi	Yes (literally: near)
mâi glâi	No (literally: not near)

mŏr gèhng mái	Is the doctor good?
gèhng	Yes (literally: good)
mâi gèhng	No (literally: not good)

Other common question words are:

a-rai	What?
mêuar-rai	When?
têe nǎi	Where?
an nǎi	Which?
krai	Who?
tam-mai	Why?

All of these words are used at the end of a sentence to make it a question. For example:

kun chêur a-rai	What is your name?
pŏm/di-chán chêur joh	My name is Jo
káo Pai gàp krai	Who is he/she going with?
káo Pai gàp joh	He/she is going with Jo
káo Pai têe nǎi	Where is he/she going?
káo Pai grung-tâyp	He/she is going to Bangkok
káo séur an nǎi	Which one did he/she buy?
káo séur an nán	He/she bought that one
káo Pai grung-tâyp tam-mai	Why is he/she going to Bangkok?
káo Pai tîaw	He/she is going for a holiday
káo glàp mar mêuar-rai	When did he/she return?
káo glàp mar mêuar warn née	He/she returned yesterday

19

Culture

▋ The Tourist Authority of Thailand (TAT) publishes a useful leaflet on do's and don'ts in Thailand, which can be obtained from any TAT offices abroad or in Thailand itself. Cultural sensitivities should be observed while you are visiting the country, so as not to cause offence.

The monarchy

The monarchy is highly revered in Thailand and criticism of the institution or members of the royal family can lead to serious trouble. Do not attempt to discuss the monarchy with Thais, as this may cause offence.

Banknotes and coins bear the figure of the Thai king, so treat them with respect. For example, if you drop any, do not try to stop them from blowing or rolling away by stamping on them with your foot. You will be in serious trouble if Thais see you doing this.

Religion

Buddhism is the national religion and more than 90% of Thais call themselves Buddhist. Temples, Buddha images and monks should therefore be treated with respect.

You should behave respectfully while visiting temples. If in doubt, do as the locals do, such as dressing neatly and taking your shoes off in certain parts of the temples. Buddha images are sacred objects, so avoid posing in front of them for pictures and do not climb on them.

Monks are forbidden to have any physical contact with women, so female visitors should make certain that they do not accidentally touch or even brush against monks.

Greetings

The traditional Thai form of greeting is a *wai* – the gesture of placing the palms together and raising them to a level just below the chin; this form of greeting should be returned. A person of lower age or inferior status should *wai* first. While Thais do not expect foreigners to be familiar with this gesture, they will appreciate it if you are able to perform it.

Polite language

Generally, Thais address each other using their first name with the title *'kun'* , often written as 'Khun' in other transliteration systems and written as คุณ in Thai, in front of it to show politeness. **"Khun"** is the Thai equivalent of Mr, Mrs or Miss. It also means "you" in a face-to-face conversation. So if you are talking or referring to a Mr Pisit Sakulthai, you should address him as 'Khun Pisit' and not 'Khun Sakulthai'.

For referring to themselves, Thais will use *'pǒm'* if they are male and *'di-chán'* if they are female. These two words are the equivalent of "I" in English. The word for 'he', 'she' or 'they' is *'káo'*.

To express politeness, Thais use a particle at the end of sentences, statements or questions for which there is no equivalent in English. Thus men will add the word *'kráp'* and women will say *'kâ'* or *'ká'*. For women, it is slightly more complicated as *'kâ'* is used when the sentence is a statement and *'ká'* when it is a question.

kráp and **kâ** can also be used on their own to convey a sense of agreement or acknowledgement, i.e. to mean 'yes'. For example:

Pai gin kâo mái	*Shall we go and eat?*
kráp/kâ	*Yes*
chôrp ar-hǎrn tai mái	*Do you like Thai food?*
kráp/kâ	*Yes*

There are two ways of saying 'thank you' in Thai and several ways of saying 'please'. The word for 'thank you' is either *kòrp kun* or *kòrp jai* depending on whether the person whom you are addressing is a social inferior, equal or superior to you. *kòrp kun* is the safer phrase to choose since this is applicable in all contexts, whereas *kòrp jai* is normally used for servants, children, shop assistants etc.

If someone uses the word *kòrp kun* to you, your automatic response should be to say *mâi Pehn rai* which means 'never mind', 'don't mention it' or 'you're welcome'.

A number of different words can be used to indicate the English 'please'. When you are asking for something, in the sense of 'please can I have', this is conveyed by the word *kǒr* at the beginning of the sentence. If you want to make this more polite, you can add the word *nòy* to the end of the sentence. For example:

kǒr kâo pàt/kǒr kâo pàt nòy	Please can I have some fried rice?
kǒr bia/kǒr bia nòy	Please can I have some beer?

There are two more formal words for 'please' that you might hear in official announcements, for example when travelling on an aeroplane. They are *Pròht* and *ga-rú-nar*. You might hear them in the following contexts:

Pròht sârp wâr rao jà Pai těuhng grung-tâyp nai nèuhng chûa-mohng Please be informed that we shall arrive in Bangkok in an hour's time

ga-rú-nar rát kěhm-kàt   Please fasten your seat belts

You do not need to use *Pròht* and *ga-rú-nar* yourselves. It is sufficient that you understand them when they are addressed to you.

Personal conduct

Thais show respect to older or more senior people who are seated by not talking to them while standing. You are advised to sit down either on a seat or on the floor. This is determined by how the elderly person is sitting. If the person is seated, you can sit either on a seat or on the floor, but you should not use a seat if the person sits down on the floor. In this case, you are expected to sit on the floor as well. It will also be appreciated if you make a gesture of bending forward a little when passing older or more senior people who are seated.

For Thais, the feet are the lowest part of the body, physically and spiritually, so don't point your feet at people or point at things with your feet. You can unintentionally cause offence by doing so. In the same context, the head is regarded as the highest part of the body, so don't touch Thais on the head.

Dress

Appearance is very important in Thailand and Thais take great care over the way they dress. It is advisable for Westerners to dress in a respectful way if you do not want to be frowned upon by Thais.

Beach attire and shorts are not considered appropriate for trips into town and are not welcomed in government offices.

Tipping

Tipping is not a normal practice in Thailand, although in expensive hotels and restaurants, you are expected to leave a small amount of money. It is entirely at your discretion whether or how much you want to leave behind as a tip.

Farang

Thais refer to all white people/Westerners as *farang* and the word is used very frequently. Generally Thais have a good deal of respect for Westerners so if you hear people referring to you as *farang* it is not intended to be rude and there is no need to be offended. It's likely that the word comes from the first Thai attempts to say the word 'France' or 'français' since the French were among the first Westerners to visit Thailand (then Siam) in the seventeenth century.

Keep your cool

As in most parts of Asia, anger and displays of emotion generally get you nowhere in Thailand. In any argument or dispute, losing one's temper or being directly critical are regarded as threats, so remember, the rule is to keep your cool.

Information extras

Ninety-nine per cent of buildings in Thailand call their lowest floor *"chán lârng"* or the 'ground floor' with the next floor up as *"chán sŏrng"* or the 'second floor'. 'Chán lârng' may be shown on the board or in a lift (in the case of an office building) as either 'G' or '1'. In the case of a two-storey house, the upper floor is normally called *"chán bon"* or 'upstairs'.

All-purpose phrases

Hello	sa-wàt-dee
Goodbye	lar-gòrn
See you	láirw jer gan
Yes	kráp/kâ *or* châi
No	mâi kráp/kâ *or* mâi châi
Yes, please	ao kráp/kâ

No, thank you	mâi ao kráp/kâ
Thank you (very much)	kòrp kun (mârk)
You're welcome/My pleasure	mâi Pehn rai
It doesn't matter	mâi Pehn rai
Excuse me	kŏr tôht
Sorry/My apologies	kŏr tôht
Help!	chûay dûay
Please call the police	chûay rîak Tam-rùat dûay
I don't know	mâi róo
I don't understand	mâi kâo-jai
I don't speak Thai	pôot tai mâi Pehn
I speak very little Thai	pôot tai mâi gèhng
Can you repeat that?	chûay pôot sám dâi mái
Slowly, please	pôot chár-chár kráp/kâ
Can you write it down?	chûay kĭan hâi nòy
… in English	… Pehn par-săr ang-grìt
… in Thai	… Pehn par-săr tai
Do you speak English?	pôot ang-grìt dâi mái
Is there anyone who speaks English?	mee krai pôot ang-grìt dâi bârng
What is this?	nêe a-rai
How do you say it in Thai?	par-săr tai rîak wâr a-rai
Is/Are there (any) …?	mee … mái
Do you have …?	mee … mái
Where is/are …?	… yòo têe năi
Where are the toilets?	hôrng nárm yòo têe năi
What time …?	… gèe mohng
How much is it?	tâo-rài
Can I/we …?/Is it possible to …?	… dâi mái
What is the matter?	gèrt a-rai kêuhn
It's (very) delicious	a-ròy (mârk)
It's fun/It's enjoyable	sa-nùk

25

Numbers

■ Although universal numerals are widely used in Thailand, you may come across numbers which are in Thai script, especially on official documents. Both types of numerals appear on Thai banknotes and coins.

Cardinals

0	sŏon	๐	ศูนย์
1	nèuhng	๑	หนึ่ง
2	sŏrng	๒	สอง
3	sărm	๓	สาม
4	sèe	๔	สี่
5	hâr	๕	ห้า
6	hòk	๖	หก
7	jèht	๗	เจ็ด
8	Pàirt	๘	แปด
9	gâo	๙	เก้า
10	sìp	๑๐	สิบ
11	sìp-èht	๑๑	สิบเอ็ด
12	sìp-sŏrng	๑๒	สิบสอง
13	sìp-sărm	๑๓	สิบสาม
14	sìp-sèe	๑๔	สิบสี่
15	sìp-hâr	๑๕	สิบห้า

16	sìp-hòk	๑๖	สิบหก
17	sìp-jèht	๑๗	สิบเจ็ด
18	sìp-Pàirt	๑๘	สิบแปด
19	sìp-gâo	๑๙	สิบเก้า
20	yêe-sìp	๒๐	ยี่สิบ
21	yêe-sìp-èht	๒๑	ยี่สิบเอ็ด
22	yêe-sìp-sörng	๒๒	ยี่สิบสอง
30	särm-sìp	๓๐	สามสิบ
31	särm-sìp-èht	๓๑	สามสิบเอ็ด
32	särm-sìp-sörng	๓๒	สามสิบสอง
40	sèe-sìp	๔๐	สี่สิบ
50	hâr-sìp	๕๐	ห้าสิบ
60	hòk-sìp	๖๐	หกสิบ
70	jèht-sìp	๗๐	เจ็ดสิบ
80	Pàirt-sìp	๘๐	แปดสิบ
90	gâo-sìp	๙๐	เก้าสิบ
100	nèuhng róy	๑๐๐	หนึ่งร้อย
101	nèuhng róy èht	๑๐๑	หนึ่งร้อยเอ็ด
102	nèuhng róy sörng	๑๐๒	หนึ่งร้อยสอง
110	nèuhng róy sìp	๑๑๐	หนึ่งร้อยสิบ
200	sörng róy	๒๐๐	สองร้อย
300	särm róy	๓๐๐	สามร้อย
1000	nèuhng pan	๑๐๐๐	หนึ่งพัน
2000	sörng pan	๒๐๐๐	สองพัน
10,000	nèuhng mèurn	๑๐๐๐๐	หนึ่งหมื่น
20,000	sörng mèurn	๒๐๐๐๐	สองหมื่น

| 100,000 | nèuhng săirn | ๑๐๐๐๐๐ | หนึ่งแสน |
| 1,000,000 | nèuhng lárn | ๑๐๐๐๐๐๐ | หนึ่งล้าน |

Ordinals

1st	têe nèuhng	ที่หนึ่ง
2nd	têe sŏrng	ที่สอง
3rd	têe sărm	ที่สาม
4th	têe sèe	ที่สี่
5th	têe hâr	ที่ห้า
6th	têe hòk	ที่หก
7th	têe jèht	ที่เจ็ด
8th	têe Pàirt	ที่แปด
9th	têe gâo	ที่เก้า
10th	têe sìp	ที่สิบ

Sometimes, in conversation, Thais may refer to 'the first' as 'แรก', so please keep this in mind.

Useful words

plus/add	bùak
minus/subtract	lóp
multiply	koon
divide	hǎrn
equal to	tâo gàp *or* Pehn

Time and the calendar

▌ Thais tell the time in three ways: by the official 24-hour clock, by the semi-formal system and by the informal system. You will probably encounter the latter two during most of your stay in Thailand. The 24-hour stystem is used in formal announcements such as on the radio and at bus and railway stations and airports.

▌ Thailand uses the Buddhist Era rather than the Christian year. This is calculated by adding 543 to the A.D. year. Thus 1995 A.D. becomes 2538 B.E.

Days – wan – วัน

Sunday	wan ar-tít	วันอาทิตย์
Monday	wan jan	วันจันทร์
Tuesday	wan ang-karn	วันอังคาร
Wednesday	wan pút	วันพุธ
Thursday	wan pá-réuh-hàt	วันพฤหัส
Friday	wan sùk	วันศุกร์
Saturday	wan săo	วันเสาร์

Months – deuarn – เดือน

January	má-ga-rar-kom	มกราคม
February	gum-par-pan	กุมภาพันธ์
March	mee-nar-kom	มีนาคม
April	may-săr-yon	เมษายน
May	préuht-sa-par-kom	พฤษภาคม
June	mí-tù-nar-yon	มิถุนายน

29

July	ga-rá-ga-dar-kom	กรกฎาคม
August	sĭng-hăr-kom	สิงหาคม
September	gan-yar-yon	กันยายน
October	Tù-lar-kom	ตุลาคม
November	préuht-sa-jì-gar-yon	พฤศจิกายน
December	tan-war-kom	ธันวาคม

Seasons

spring	réuh-doo bai-mái plì
summer	réuh-doo rórn
autumn	réuh-doo bai-mái rûang
winter	réuh-doo năo
rainy season	nâr fŏn
hot season	nâr rórn
cool season	nâr năo

Telling the time

midnight	tĭang keurn
1 a.m.	Tee nèuhng
2 a.m.	Tee sŏrng
3 a.m.	Tee sărm
4 a.m.	Tee sèe
5 a.m.	Tee hâr
6 a.m.	hòk mohng cháo
7 a.m.	jèht mohng (*semi-formal*)
	mohng cháo (*informal*)
8 a.m.	Pàirt mohng (*semi-formal*)
	sŏrng mohng cháo (*informal*)

9 a.m.	gâo mohng (*semi-formal*)
	sărm mohng cháo (*informal*)
10 a.m.	sìp mohng (semi-formal)
	sèe mohng cháo (informal)
11 a.m.	sìp-èht mohng (semi-formal)
	hâr mohng cháo (informal)
midday/noon	tîang or tîang wan
1 p.m.	bài mohng
2 p.m.	bài sŏrng mohng
3 p.m.	bài sărm mohng
4 p.m.	bài sèe mohng (*semi-formal*)
	sèe mohng yehn (*informal*)
5 p.m.	bài hâr mohng (*semi-formal*)
	hâr mohng yehn (*informal*)
6 p.m.	hòk mohng yehn
7 p.m.	nèuhng tûm
8 p.m.	sŏrng tûm
9 p.m.	sărm tûm
10 p.m.	sèe tûm
11 p.m.	hâr tûm
a quarter past ...	... sìp-hâr
twenty past ...	... yêe-sìp
half past ...	... krêuhng
9.15 a.m.	gâo mohng sìp-hâr
10.20 p.m.	sèe tûm yêe-sìp
1.30 p.m.	bài mohng krêuhng
a quarter to ...	... sèe-sìp-hâr
ten to ...	... hâr-sìp
twenty to ...	... sèe-sìp
6.45 a.m.	hòk mohng sèe-sìp-hâr
11.50 a.m.	sìp-èht mohng hâr-sìp
4.40 p.m.	bài sèe mohng sèe-sìp

24-hour clock system

The structure of the 24-hour clock system is as follows:

number of hours + **nar-lí-gar** + number of minutes + **nar-tee**

0500 hrs.	hâr nar-lí-gar
0910 hrs.	gâo nar-lí-gar sìp nar-tee
1115 hrs.	sìp-èht nar-lí-gar sìp-hâr nar-tee
1330 hrs.	sìp-sǎrm nar-lí-gar sǎrm-sìp nar-tee
1743 hrs.	sìp-jèht nar-lí-gar sèe-sìp-sǎrm nar-tee
2045 hrs.	yêe-sìp nar-lí-gar sèe-sìp-hâr nar-tee

Saying the date

10 January	wan têe sìp má-ga-rar-kom
21 August	wan têe yêe-sìp-èht sǐng-här-kom
Thursday 2 June	wan pá-réuh-hàt têe sǒrng mí-tù-nar-yon
Sunday 3 February	wan ar-tít têe sǎrm gum-par-pan
A.D.	kor-sǒr
B.E.	por-sǒr

Useful words

day	wan
date	wan têe
week	ar-tít or sàp-dar
month	deuarn
year	Pee
century	sàt-Ta-wát
hour	chûa-mohng
minute	nar-tee

second	wí-nar-tee
a quarter of an hour	sìp-hâr nar-tee
half an hour	krêuhng chûa-mohng
three quarters of an hour	sèe-sìp-hâr nar-tee
on Monday	wan jan
on Sundays/every Sunday	túk wan ar-tít
in January	deuarn má-ga-rar-kom
during the winter	Torn nâr näo or Torn réuh-doo näo
at the beginning of …	Torn Tôn …
at the end of …	Torn Plai …
in the middle of …	Torn glarng …
… March	… deuarn mee-nar-kom
… the week	… ar-tít
… the month	… deuarn
… the year	… Pee
at the weekend	Torn sùt sàp-dar
every day	túk wan
all day	táng wan
the next day	wan rûng kêuhn
last …	… têe láirw
next …	… nâr
this …	… née
… Tuesday	wan ang-karn …
… April	deuarn may-sǎr-yon …
… week	ar-tít …
… month	deuarn …
… year	Pee …
… weekend	sùt sàp-dar …
today	wan née
yesterday	mêuar warn née
tomorrow	prûng née

33

the day before yesterday	warn seurn née
the day after tomorrow	wan ma-reurn née
this ...	... née
yesterday ...	... warn née
tomorrow ...	... prûng née
... morning	cháo ...
... afternoon	bài ...
... evening	yehn ...
Monday morning	cháo wan jan
Wednesday afternoon	bài wan pút
Friday evening	yehn wan sùk
Sunday night	keurn wan ar-tít
tonight	keurn née
last night	keurn warn née
tomorrow night	keurn prûng née
before Saturday	gòrn wan são
after Wednesday	loei wan pút Pai láirw
until Friday	jon těuhng wan sùk
in the ...	Torn ...
... early morning	... cháo Tròo
... morning	... cháo
... late morning	... sǎi
... afternoon	... bài
... late afternoon	... yehn
... early evening	... hǔa kâm
... evening	... kâm
... late evening	... dèuhk
in/during the daytime	Torn glarng wan
in/during the night time or at night	Torn glarng keurn
at ...	Torn ...
... 8 o'clock	... Pàirt mohng

34

... noon	... tîang
in ...	èek ...
... an hour's time	... nèuhng chûa-mohng
... three days' time	... sǎrm wan
... five weeks' time	... hâr ar-tít
... seven months' time	... jèht deuarn
... ago	... gòrn
half an hour ...	krêuhng chûa-mohng ...
four days ...	sèe wan ...
a fortnight ...	sǒrng ar-tít ...
ten years ...	sìp Pee ...
on time	Trong way-lar
early	rehw
late	chár/sǎi
soon	èek-mâi-chár
now/at the moment	dǐaw-née
earlier on	gòrn-nâr-née
later on	tee-lǎng

You may want to say

Excuse me!	kǒr tôht kráp/kâ
What time is it?	gèe mohng láirw kráp/ká
(At) what time ...?	... Torn gèe mohng
When ...?	... mêuar rài
What day is it today?	wan née wan a-rai
What is the date today?	wan née wan têe tâo rài

35

General conversation

▌ See "Culture" for general greetings and polite language.

▌ Although **'sa-wàt-dee'** is the general expression for "hello", and is used throughout the day and night, the typical Thai greeting does not mean "hello", or even "how are you?", but rather "where are you going?", or "where have you been?". This is a general reflection of the Thai attitude to life, which is 'to have fun' or **'sa-nùk'**. Thais do not say 'good night' to each other as such. They tend to say the equivalent of 'I'll go to bed now'.

▌ To most Thai people, a Briton, whether he or she is English, Scottish, Welsh or Irish, will be known as an Englishman or Englishwoman. So if you are not English, do accept it as a way of life and try not to be annoyed. Even the British Embassy calls itself 'the English Embassy' when translated into Thai.

▌ In general, to answer 'yes' to a question you repeat the verb in the question and to answer 'no' you use the word **'mâi'** in front of the verb. **'Mâi'** is a negative word in Thai. (See "Grammar" Section)

▌ To turn a statement into a question, generally you just add **'châi mái'** at the end of the statement. To answer a question with a **'châi mái'** ending, you say **'châi'** for 'yes' and **'mâi châi'** for 'no'.

You may want to say

Greetings and goodbyes

Hello	sa-wàt-dee
Goodbye	lar gòrn
See you	láirw jer gan
Good night (*I'll go to bed now*)	Pai norn lâ ná

How are you?	Pehn yàrng rai bârng
Fine, thanks	sa-bai dee
And you?	láirw kun lâ
Where have you been?	Pai năi mar
I've been to …	Pai … mar
Where are you going?	jà Pai năi
I'm going to …	jà Pai …

General phrases

Yes	kráp/kâ *or* châi
No	mâi kráp/kâ *or* mâi châi
Yes, please	ao kráp/kâ
No, thank you	mâi ao kráp/kâ
Please *(asking for something)*	kŏr
Please *(asking someone to do something)*	chûay
Thank you (very much)	kòrp kun (mârk)
You're welcome/My pleasure	mâi Pehn rai
Excuse me	kŏr tôht
Sorry (apology)	kŏr tôht
OK	Tòk long
Let's go	Pai gan tèuh
I don't speak Thai	pôot tai mâi Pehn
Do you speak English?	pôot ang-grìt dâi mái
I don't understand	mâi kâo-jai
Could you repeat that?	chûay pôot sám dûay dâi mái
Slowly, please	pôot chár-chár kráp/kâ
Can you write it down?	chûay kĭan hâi nòy
… in English	… Pehn par-săr ang-grìt
… in Thai	… Pehn par-săr tai
I like …	pŏm/dì-chán chôrp …
I don't like …	pŏm/dì-chán mâi chôrp …

37

Do you like it?	chôrp mái
Do you like …?	chôrp … mái
I love you	pŏm/di-chán rák kun

Introductions

My name is …	pŏm/di-chán chêur …
This is … (person)	kon née chêur …
This is Larry	kon née chêur lair-rêe
This is Jane	kon née chêur jayn
What's your name?	kun chêur a-rai

Talking about yourself

I am … (nationality)	pŏm/di-chán Pehn kon …
… American	… a-may-rí-gan
… British	… ang-grìt
… French	… fa-ràng-sàyt
… German	… yer-ra-man
We come from London	rao mar jàrk lon-don
I am a student	pŏm/di-chán Pehn nák-sèuhk-săr
I work in/for a bank	pŏm/di-chán tam-ngarn ta-nar-karn
I work in London	pŏm/di-chán tam-ngarn têe lon-don
I am … (marital status)	pŏm/di-chán …
… single	… Pehn sòht
… married	… tàirng-ngarn láirw
… divorced	… yàr láirw
… a widower	… Pehn pôr mâi
… a widow	… Pehn mâir mâi
I am 30 years old	pŏm/di-chán ar-yú sărm-sìp
He/she is 25 years old	káo ar-yú yêe-sìp-hâr

Talking about Thailand

I like … (very much)	pŏm/di-chán chôrp … (mârk)
… Thailand	… meuarng tai
… Thai food	… ar-hărn tai
… Thai people	… kon tai
Thailand is (very) beautiful	meuarng tai sŭay (mârk)
Thai women are very beautiful	pôo-yĭng tai sŭay mârk
It's my first time in Thailand	mar meuarng tai kráng râirk
I often come to Thailand	mar meuarng tai bòy

Good wishes

Happy Birthday	sùk-săn wan-gèrt
Happy New Year	sa-wàt-dee Pee mài
Good Luck	kŏr hâi chôhk dee
Congratulations	yin-dee dûay
Enjoy yourself/yourselves	kŏr hâi sa-nùk

Weather

The weather's (very) good	ar-gàrt dee (mârk)
The weather's (very) bad	ar-gàrt yâir (mârk)
It's (very) hot	ar-gàrt rórn (mârk)
It's fine	ar-gàrt gam-lang dee
It's very windy	lom rairng mârk
Is it going to rain?	fŏn jà Tòk mái

Questions about yourself

chêur a-rai	What's your name?
mar jàrk nǎi	Where are you from?
mar kon diaw rěur Plào	Are you travelling alone?
ar-yú tâo rài	How old are you?
tam-ngarn a-rai	What do you do?
rian nǎng-sěur a-rai	What are you studying?
Tàirng-ngarn rěur yang	Are you married?
mee lôok gèe kon	How many children have you got?
mee pêe nórng gèe kon	How many brothers and sisters have you got?
jà Pai têe nǎi	Where are you heading for?
pák têe nǎi	Where are you staying?

Talking about Thailand

pôot tai dâi mái	Can you speak Thai?
chôrp ... mái	Do you like ...?
... meuarng tai ...	... Thailand
... ar-hǎrn tai ...	... Thai food
... kon tai ...	... Thai people
mar kráng râirk rěur Plào	Is this your first visit to Thailand?
pôot tai gèhng nêe	Your Thai is very good!

Arrival and customs

▌ Most visitors arrive at Bangkok International Airport, or **Don Muang** as it is known locally, though some may fly direct into Phuket or Chiang Mai airports and some will come by train from Malaysia to southern Thailand. Whichever way you arrive, the formalities are straightforward. You'll need a valid passport and if you have not acquired a tourist visa from a Thai embassy or consulate prior to arrival in Thailand, you should be allowed to stay in Thailand up to a maximum of 30 days, provided that you have an onward or return ticket. Please note that in this case, no extension is permitted. If you stay longer, you will be fined for each day you have overstayed.

▌ Immigration and customs officers at the port of entry will ask you some questions in English, so you may not need to say anything in Thai. All signs in the three airports above and at the Thai-Malaysian immigration checkpoint are in both Thai and English.

Useful words

airport	sa-nǎrm bin
bag/luggage/suitcase	gra-Pǎo
customs	sǔn-lá-gar-gorn
immigration	Trùat kon kâo meuarng
passport	párt-sa-Pòrt/nǎng-sěur dern-tarng
passport control	Trùat long Trar nǎng-sěur dern-tarng

You may want to say

I am here ...	pǒm/di-chán ...
... on holiday	... mar tîaw

... on business	... mar tú-rá
... on my own	... mar kon diaw
... with my family	... mar gàp krôrp-krua
... with my friend	... mar gàp pêuarn
I have something to declare	pŏm/di-chán mee kŏrng Tôrng sa-dairng
I have a receipt for this	pŏm/di-chán mee bai-sèht
That's ...	nân ...
... (not) mine	... (mâi châi) kŏrng pŏm/di-chán
... (not) ours	... (mâi châi) kŏrng rao
Where can I get a taxi to town?	jà rîak rót táihk-sêe kâo meuarng dâi têe năi

You may hear

Immigration

kŏr doo párt-sa-Pòrt	Your passport, please
mar tam a-rai	What is the purpose of your visit?
jà yòo gèe wan	How long are you staying?
mar kon diaw rěur Plào	Are you travelling alone?

Customs

chûay Pèrt gra-Păo dûay	Please open your bag/suitcase
mee gra-Păo èurn èek mái	Do you have any other luggage?
mee bai-sèht rěur Plào	Have you got a receipt for this?
kŏrng kun rěur Plào	Does this belong to you?
an née Pehn kŏrng krai	To whom does this belong?
Tarm pŏm/di-chán mar tarng née	Come with me
ror yòo Trong née	Wait here

Directions

▌General street maps of Thailand's main cities are available from most of the bookshops which sell English-language materials. There are a few such bookshops in Bangkok and in the main tourist cities such as Chiang Mai, Phuket and Pattaya.

Remember that there is no standardized form of transliterating Thai names (of streets, places or even people) into English. And the form you come across certainly won't be the one that is used here! If you are looking for a particular address, have it written down in Thai.

Useful signs

ถนน	ta-nŏn	road/street
ซอย	soy	side street
ตรอก	Tròrk	alley way
ห้ามเข้า	hârm kâo	no entry
ห้ามจอด	hârm jòrt	no parking
หยุดตรวจ	yùt Trùat	stop! checkpoint!
ระวัง สุนัข	rá-wang sù-nák	beware of the dog

Useful words

address	têe yôo
crossroads where …	
3 streets meet	sărm yâirk
4 streets meet	sèe yâirk
5 streets meet	hâr yâirk
left	sái

right	kwăr
map	păirn-têe
pedestrian/zebra crossing	tarng már-lai

You may want to say

Excuse me	kŏr tôht kráp/kâ
I am lost	pŏm/di-chán lŏng tarng
Where is ...?	... Pai tarng năi
... this address	bârn née ...
... this road/street	ta-nŏn née ...
... the bus station	sa-tăr-nee kŏn sòng ...
... the railway station	sa-tăr-nee rót fai ...
Is there a ... around here?	tăihw née mee ... mái
... bank ...	... ta-nar-karn ...
... bus stop ...	... Pâi rót may ...
... chemist ...	... rárn kăi yar ...
... petrol station ...	... Pám nám-man ...
... police station ...	... sa-tăr-nee Tam-rùat ...
... post office ...	... Prai-sa-nee ...
... toilet ...	... hôrng nárm ...
Is this the right way to ...?	tarng née Pai ... chái mái
How do I get to ...?	jà Pai ... dâi yàrng-rai
Speak slowly, please	pôot chár-chár nòy kráp/kâ
Say it again, please	pôot èek tee dâi kráp/kâ
Can you show me on the map?	chûay chée bon păirn-têe dûay kráp/kâ
Is it far?	yòo glai mái
Can I get there on foot?	dern Pai dâi mái
Is there a bus?	mee rót may Pai mái

You may hear

loei mar láirw	You've gone past it
mar pìt tarng	You've gone the wrong way
Tôrng glàp Pai tarng gào	You'll have to go back the same way
Trong Pai	Straight on
Pai tarng née	This way
Pai tarng nán	That way
têe nêe/Trong née	Here
têe nân/Trong nán	There
líaw sái	Turn left
líaw kwăr	Turn right
yòo tarng sái	It's on the left
yòo tarng kwăr	It's on the right
líaw sái yâirk râirk	The first on the left
líaw kwăr yâirk râirk	The first on the right
líaw sái yâirk têe sŏrng	The second on the left
líaw kwăr yâirk têe sŏrng	The second on the right
líaw sái yâirk têe sărm	The third on the left
líaw kwăr yâirk têe sărm	The third on the right
yòo fàng née	It's on this side of the road
yòo fàng nán	It's on that side for the road
yòo loei … Pai (nòy)	(Just) Past …
… sa-parn loy …	… the flyover
… wát …	… the temple
… fai-kîaw-fai-dairng	… the traffic lights
yòo gòrn tĕuhng …	Before …
yòo Trong kârm …	Opposite …
yòo glâi gàp …	Next/Close to …
yòo kârng nâr …	In front of …
yòo kârng lăng …	Behind …

yòo hǔa mum ta-nǒn	At the corner of the street
yòo hǔa ta-nǒn	At the beginning of the street
yòo sùt ta-nǒn	At the end of the street
yòo Pàrk soy	At the beginning of the side street
yòo cherng sa-parn	At the foot of the bridge
yòo rim mâir-nárm	At the river side
yòo rim klorng	At the canal side
yòo glai	It's a long way away
yòo mâi glai	It's not far away
yòo glâi kâir née	It's quite close
… sìp nar-tee tĕuhng	It's ten minutes away …
dern …	… on foot
nâng rót …	… by car
yòo glai hâr gi-loh	It's five kilometres away
yòo …	It's on the …
… chán lârng	… first floor
… chán sǒrng	… second floor
… chán bon sùt	… top floor
yòo chán bon	It's upstairs
yòo chán lârng	It's downstairs
yòo …	It's the …
… Pra-Too râirk	… first door
… Pra-Too têe sǎrm	… third door
… Pra-Too sùt-tái	… last door

Air travel

▌ Thai Airways International (THAI) operates most domestic air services within Thailand. A small carrier called Bangkok Airways is licensed to operate on certain routes, such as to the island resort of Koh Samui in the south. Some of THAI's domestic flights to the southern towns of Hat Yai and Phuket continue on to Penang and Kuala Lumpur in Malaysia, and to Singapore.

▌ At airports and airline offices, you'll generally find someone who speaks English, but be prepared to say a few things in Thai.

▌ Signs at most airports and in all THAI and Bangkok Airways aircraft are printed in both Thai and English.

▌ Airport departure tax is payable on both international and domestic flights.

▌ Bangkok is a major centre for international flights throughout Asia. Bankok and some of the main tourist cities, such as Chiang Mai, Pattaya and Phuket, are major centres for buying discounted airline tickets; but be warned that some agents are not reputable, so do check carefully before purchasing.

Useful signs

สนามบิน	sa-nărm bin	airport
ในประเทศ	nai Pra-tâyt	domestic
ระหว่างประเทศ	rá-wàrng Pra-tâyt	international
ขาเข้า	kăr kâo	arrival
ขาออก	kăr òrk	departure
ทางเข้า	tarng kâo	entrance
ทางออก	tarng òrk	gate *(boarding)* exit *(way out)*

ประชาสัมพันธ์	Pra-char sǎm-pan	information
ห้ามสูบบุหรี่	hârm sòop bu-rèe	no smoking
ห้องสุขา	hôrng sù-kǎr	toilets
ชาย/ สุภาพบุรุษ	chai/sù-pârp bu-rùt	gentlemen
หญิง/ สุภาพสตรี	yǐng/sù-pârp sàt-Tree	ladies

Useful words

aircraft	krêuarng bin	final call	Pra-gàrt kráng sùt-tái
delay	sǐa way-lar	flight	tîaw bin
departure tax	kâr tam-niam sa-nǎrm bin	ticket	Tǔa

You may want to say

Information

Is there a flight from … to …?	mee tîaw bin jàrk … Pai … mái
Which airlines fly to …?	sǎi-garn-bin nǎi bin Pai … bârng
How many flights … are there?	… gèe tîaw
… a day …	wan lá …
… a week …	ar-tít lá …
Do you have a timetable for flights to …?	mee Tar-rarng bin Pai … mái
What time …?	… gèe mohng
What time is … to Phuket?	krêuarng bin Pai poo-gèht … òrk gèe mohng
… the first flight …	… tîaw râirk …
… the next flight …	… tîaw Tòr-Pai …
… the last flight …	… tîaw sùt-tái …
What time does it arrive?	Pai tĕuhng gèe mohng
Is it a direct flight?	bin Trong mái

48

Do I have to change planes?	Tôrng Plìan krêuarng mái
Where do I have to change planes?	Plìan krêuarng têe nǎi

Tickets

I'd like to buy an airline ticket to …	kŏr séur Tŭa krêuarng bin Pai … kráp/kâ
One seat	nèuhng têe
Two seats	sŏrng têe
Single	tîaw-diaw
Return	Pai-glàp
First-class	chán nèuhng
Business-class	chán tú-ra-gìt
Economy-class	chán Pra-yàt
For the 10 o'clock flight	tîaw sìp mohng
I want to … my reservation	kŏr … wan dern tarng
… change …	… Plìan …
… cancel …	… yók lêrk …
I want to reconfirm my flight	kŏr kon-ferm Tŭa
What is my flight number?	tîaw bin a-rai
What time do I have to check in?	Tôrng chéhk-in gèe mohng
How do I get to the airport?	Pai sa-nǎrm bin dâi yàrng rai

Checking in

Is there a delay?	krêuarng sǐa way-lar mái
How long do I have to wait?	Tôrng ror narn tâo-rài
I'd like …	kŏr …
… a seat by the window	… têe nâng Tìt nâr-Tàrng
… an aisle seat	… têe nâng Tìt tarng dern
Smoking	sòop bu-rèe
Non-smoking	mâi sòop bu-rèe
Which gate is it?	tarng òrk ber a-rai

Arrival

My luggage isn't here	gra-Pǎo kǒrng pǒm/di-chán mâi mar dûay
Where is the … desk?	Tó … yòo têe nǎi
… THAI airlines …	… sǎi-garn-bin tai …
Is there a bus to town?	mee rót may kâo meuarng mái
Where can I get a taxi?	rîak rót táihk-sêe dâi têe nǎi

You may hear

Check in

sòop bu-rèe mái kráp/ká	Smoking or non-smoking
kêuhn krêuarng way-lar …	Board at … (time)
tarng òrk ber …	Gate number …
kǒr Tǔa kráp/kâ	Your ticket, please
kǒr párt-sa-Pòrt kráp/kâ	Your passport, please

Boarding

Pra-gàrt kráng sùt-tái	Final call
kǒrng tîaw bin têe …	For flight number …
kǒr bàt kêuhn krêuarng kráp/kâ	Your boarding card, please

Arrival

gra-Pǎo bàirp nǎi	What does your luggage look like?
sěe a-rai	What colour is it?
yêe-hôr a-rai	Any brand name on it?
mee Tǔa gra-Pǎo mái	Do you have the reclaim tag/ticket?
gròrk form née kráp/kâ	Fill in this form, please

Travelling by train

▌ The State Railway of Thailand (SRT) has been computerized over the past few years and reservations can now be made at major stations in Bangkok and provincial cities along the network routes. Even so, travelling by train in Thailand is usually slower than taking the bus.

▌ Thai trains usually have three classes – first, second and third. Unless you have no choice, you should avoid travelling third-class as you will find the seats rather hard. For long-distance travel, sleepers are available in first- and second-class and you have a choice in second-class between air-conditioned carriages and those with a fan. Carriages with a fan tend to get rather stuffy at night when the train windows are closed, but they are slightly cheaper. You also have a choice in second-class sleepers between an upper or a lower berth. Upper berths are cheaper but more cramped.

▌ There are four major routes which link Bangkok to the north, the upper north-east, the lower north-east and the south.

▌ Bangkok's main railway station is known as "Hualampong". All trains serving the four major routes leave from here. There is another terminus called "Thonburi" or "Bangkok Noi" station, situated on the Thonburi side of Bangkok, from which some trains to the south also leave. Trains to the world-famous Bridge on the River Kwai in Kanjanaburi Province also leave from Bangkok Noi station.

▌ Travelling between the south and the other three major routes will always involve a change of trains at Bangkok's Hua Lampong station.

▌ There are various types of trains, listed here from the slowest to the fastest:

Ordinary – very slow, stopping at every station;
Rapid – a faster train, not stopping at minor stations;
Express – slightly faster than the Rapid but stopping at roughly the same stations;

Special Express – faster than the Express, stopping at major stations only and with first- and second-class carriages only;

Sprinter – a recently-introduced train using UK-made rolling stock. It runs between Bangkok and some main cities. First-class air-conditioned carriages only, with meals included in the fare.

❙ There is a supplementary charge on all services apart from on the Ordinary trains. This charge varies according to the speed of the train, but is in all cases nominal.

Useful signs

สถานีรถไฟ	sa-tăr-nee rót fai	railway station
นายสถานี	nai sa-tăr-nee	stationmaster
สอบถาม	sòrp-tărm	enquiries/information
สำรองที่นั่ง	săm-rorng têe-nâng	reservations
จำหน่ายตั๋วล่วงหน้า	jam-nài Tŭa lûang-nâr	advance booking office
เดินทางวันนี้	dern tarng wan née	travelling today
ห้องขายตั๋ว	hông kăi Tŭa	ticket office
เต็ม	Tehm	full
ชานชาลา	charn char-lar	platform
ออก	òrk	departure
ถึง	tĕuhng	arrival
ห้องสุขา/ห้องน้ำ	hông sù-kăr/hông nárm	toilets
ชาย/สุภาพบุรุษ	chai/sù-pârp bu-rùt	gentlemen
หญิง/สุภาพสตรี	yĭng/sù-pârp sàt-Tree	ladies
เสีย	sĭa	out of order
ที่ฝากของ	têe fàrk kŏrng	left-luggage
เปิด	Pèrt	open
ปิด	Pìt	closed
ห้ามเข้า	hârm kâo	no entry
ห้ามสูบบุหรี่	hârm sòop bu-rèe	no smoking

Useful words

guard	nai Trùat
ticket	Tŭa
train	rót fai

You may want to say

Information

Is there a train to …?	mee rót fai Pai … mái
Do you have a timetable for trains to …?	mee Tar-rarng rót fai Pai … mái
What time …?	… gèe mohng
What time is the train to …?	rót fai Pai … òrk gèe mohng
What time is … to Chiangmai?	rót fai Pai chiang-mài … òrk gèe mohng
… the first train …	… ka-buan râirk …
… the next train …	… ka-buan Tòr-Pai …
… the last train …	… ka-buan sùt-tái …
What time does it arrive (in …)?	rót tĕuhng (…) gèe mohng
What time does the train from … arrive?	rót fai jàrk … mar tĕuhng gèe mohng
Does this train go to …?	rót fai ka-buan née Pai … mái
Does this train stop at …?	rót fai ka-buan née yùt têe … mái
Do I have to change trains?	Tôrng Plìan rót mái
Where do I have to change?	Plìan têe năi
How long does it take to get to …?	Pai … gèe chûa-mohng tĕuhng
Which platform is it for …?	Pai … charn char-lar năi
Is this the right platform for the … train?	rót fai Pai … charn char-lar née châi mái
Is this the right train for …?	rót fai ka-buan née Pai … châi mái

53

Tickets

One/Two tickets to …, please	Tŭa Pai … nèuhng/sŏrng bai kráp/kâ
Single	tĭaw-diaw
Return	Pai-glàp
First-class	chán nèuhng
Second-class	chán sŏrng
Third-class	chán sărm
For one adult	pôo-yài nèuhng kon
For two adults	pôo-yài sŏrng kon
(and) one child	(gàp) dèhk nèuhng kon
(and) two children	(gàp) dèhk sŏrng kon
For the 0700 train to …	rót fai tĭaw jèht mohng Pai …
ordinary train	rót tam-ma-dar
rapid train	rót rehw
express train	rót dùan
special express train	rót dùan pí-sàyt
sprinter	rót sa-Prín-têr
An air-conditioned compartment, please	kŏr rót air kráp/kâ
I want to buy a ticket in advance to …	kŏr séur Tŭa lûang-nâr Pai …
I want to reserve a seat	kŏr jorng têe nâng
I want to reserve a sleeper	kŏr jorng têe norn
an upper berth	chán bon
a lower berth	chán lârng
Is there a supplement?	sĭa kâr tam-niam mái
How much is it?	tâo-rài

Left-luggage

Can I leave this here?	fàrk kŏrng têe nêe dâi mái
What is the charge (for left-luggage)?	kâr fàrk tâo rài
What time do you open?	Pèrt gèe mohng
What time do you close?	Pìt gèe mohng

On the train

I have reserved a seat	pŏm/di-chán jorng têe nâng wái láirw
Excuse me	kŏr tôht kráp/kâ
May I get past/through, please	kŏr tarng nòy kráp/kâ
I think this seat is mine	têe nâng née kít wâr Pehn kŏrng pŏm/di-chán
My ticket shows …	Tŭa pŏm/di-chán bòrk wâr …
… carriage number …	… Tôo ber …
… seat number …	… têe nâng ber …
Is this seat free?	têe nâng wârng mái kráp/ká
This seat is taken	mee kon jorng láirw
Where is the dining car?	Tôo sa-biang Pai tarng nǎi
Where are the toilets?	hôrng nárm Pai tarng nǎi
Do you mind if I open the window?	kŏr Pèrt nâr-Tàrng dâi mái
Do you mind if I close the door?	kŏr Pìt Pra-Too dâi mái
Do you mind if I smoke?	kŏr sòop bu-rèe dâi mái
Where are we?	tĕuhng nǎi láirw
Are we in …?	têe nêe … châi mái
When do we arrive in …?	jà tĕuhng … gèe mohng
How long do we stop here?	jà yùt têe nêe narn tâo-rài
Can you tell me when we get to …?	tĕuhng … láirw chûay bòrk dûay
Would you mind keeping an eye on my things for me, please?	chûay doo kŏrng hâi nòy dai mái kráp/ká

55

You may hear

Information

rót òrk jèht mohng	It leaves at seven o'clock
rót tĕuhng bài sèe mohng krêuhng	It arrives at four thirty
Tôrng Plìan rót têe ...	You have to change trains at ...

Tickets

jà Pai mêuar rài/jà Pai wan năi	When do you want to travel? *(on what day)*
jà Pai gèe mohng	What time do you want to travel? *(at what hour)*
tîaw-diaw rĕur Pai-glàp	Single or return?
jà glàp mêuar rài	When do you want to return?
rót Tehm	The train is full
chán nèuhng/chán sŏrng Tehm	First-class/Second-class is full
ka-buan née mee Tàir chán nèuhng (gàp chán sŏrng)	The train is first- (and second-) class only
Tôrng sĭa kâr tam-niam ... bàrt	There is a supplement of ... baht
táng mòt ... bàrt	It's ... baht

On the train

nân têe nâng kŏrng pŏm/di-chán	That's my seat
kŏrng kun yòo Trong nán	Yours is there
kŏrng kun yòo Tôo èurn	Yours is in another carriage
tărm nai Trùat doo sî	Ask the guard

Bus and coach travel

▌ This chapter deals with long-distance buses. See City Transport for local bus services.

▌ On long-distance buses, you either pay the bus conductor on board or buy your ticket at the bus station. For air-conditioned buses on many popular routes, however, you may have to buy tickets in advance, either at the bus station or from the operator of the route concerned.

▌ Long-distances buses are run both by the government transport company (**Bor Kŏr Sŏr**) and private operators under licence from the Transport Ministry. **Bor Kŏr Sŏr** runs both ordinary buses (**rót tam-ma-dar**) equipped with fans, and air-conditioned buses (**rót air**). Privately-run buses known, as "tour" buses (**rót tua**), are air-conditioned.

▌ There may also be mini-bus services (**rót mi-ní bát**) between certain cities. These seat 10-12 passengers, are air-conditioned and cost slightly more than the buses.

▌ All cities and towns have a bus terminal, although this may only be a small parking bay by the side of the road in front of the ticket office. Bangkok has three main bus stations for all **Bor Kŏr Sŏr**'s buses and for most, if not all, of the licensed private "tour" buses.

▌ Bangkok's Northern and North-Eastern Bus Terminal is known as **Mor Chit Station** or "sa-tăr-nee mŏr-chít", the Eastern Bus Terminal as **Ekamai Station** or "sa-tăr-nee àyk-ga-mai", and the Southern Bus Terminal as **Sai Tai Station** or "sa-tăr-nee săi Tâi". All three stations have separate terminals for the ordinary buses and the air-conditioned buses so make sure you go to the right one.

▌ When travelling overnight on buses, take care of your belongings. The Tourist Authority of Thailand warns tourists travelling by bus or train not to accept food, drinks or sweets from strangers, no matter how friendly they may seem, since there have been occasional reports of travellers being drugged and robbed.

Useful signs

สถานีขนส่ง	sa-tǎr-nee kǒn-sòng	bus terminal
สอบถาม	sòrp-tǎrm	enquiry/information
ห้องขายตั๋ว	hôrng kǎi Tǔa	ticket office
จำหน่ายตั๋วล่วงหน้า	jam-nài Tǔa lûang-nâr	advanced booking
เต็ม	Tehm	full
เวลารถออก	way-lar rót òrk	departure
เวลารถเข้า	way-lar rót kâo	arrival
ห้องสุขา/ ห้องน้ำ	hôrng sù-kǎr/hôrng nárm	toilets
ชาย	chai	gentlemen
หญิง	yǐng	ladies
ห้ามสูบบุหรี่	hârm sòop bu-rèe	no smoking

Useful words

ticket	Tǔa
single	tǐaw-diaw
return	Pai-glàp

You may want to say

Information and tickets

Where is the bus terminal?	sa-tǎr-nee kǒn-sòng Pai tarng nǎi
Is there … to Chiangmai ?	mee … Pai chiang-mài mái
… a bus …	… rót
… an ordinary bus …	… rót tam-ma-dar …
… an air-conditioned bus …	… rót air …
What time is the bus to …?	rót Pai … òrk gèe mohng

What time is … to Phuket ?	rót Pai poo-gèht … òrk gèe mohng
… the first bus …	… kan râirk …
… the next bus …	… kan Tòr-Pai …
… the last bus …	… kan sùt-tái …
What time does it arrive there?	rót tĕuhng gèe mohng
What time does the bus from … arrive?	rót jàrk … mar tĕuhng gèe mohng
Where can I buy tickets?	séur Tŭa dâi têe năi
One/two tickets to …, please	Pai … nèuhng/sŏrng têe
I want to buy a ticket in advance to …	pŏm/di-chán kŏr séur Tŭa lûang-nâr Pai …
How much is it?	tâo-rài

On the bus

Is this the right bus for …?	rót kan née Pai … châi mái
Is this seat free?	têe nâng wârng mái kráp/ká
This seat is taken	mee kon jorng láirw
Could you open/close the window?	chûay Pèrt/Pìt nâr-Tàrng dâi mái
Can you tell me where to get off?	tĕuhng láirw chûay bòrk dûay
Next stop, please	jòrt Pâi nâr dûay
Excuse me, may I get past/through?	kŏr tarng dûay kráp/kâ

You may hear

rót òrk jàrk charn char-lar ber …	The bus leaves from bay number …
séur Tŭa têe nêe	Buy your ticket here
séur Tŭa bon rót	Buy your ticket on board
tîaw-diaw rĕur Pai-glàp	Single or return?
jà long rĕur Plào	Do you want to get off?
long Pâi nâr	Get off at the next stop
loei mar láirw	You've gone past it

59

City transport

▌ There are extensive bus services in Bangkok and other major cities in Thailand. Bangkok, Chiang Mai and Phitsanulok have two types of buses: **rót air** (air-conditioned) and **rót tam-ma-dar** (non-air-conditioned).

▌ You buy your ticket on board from a bus conductor and you have to buy a new ticket every time you change buses. Bangkok buses charge a flat fare, except for longer trips (usually over 10 kilometres), for which you pay a higher fare. Air-conditioned buses charge by fare stages. Bus fares in most other cities are also based on stages, so you will have to tell the bus conductor where you want to get off the bus.

▌ The route number is usually displayed at the front of the bus and the destinations are written on the side, though they will be in Thai only. Sometimes, when a bus does not go all the way to the given destination, there will be a sign on the front displaying the furthest point it goes to. This, too, is in Thai.

▌ There are riverbus services operating along the Chao Praya River in Bangkok (known as **"reuar dùan jâo prá-yar"** – Chao Praya express boat) and some canals **(klorng)** on both Pranakorn and Thonburi sides of the city. You buy your ticket on board and you have to state your destination. Most boats serving the canals on the Thonburi side are called **"reuar hǎrng yao"** – literally long-tailed boats. They charge a flat fare and you pay the boat driver at the end of your journey.

▌ In Bangkok, there are also cross-river ferries **(reuar kârm fârk)** to and from many jetties along the Chao Praya River. The fare is collected at the entrance to the jetty.

▌ Other forms of city transport include taxis, small pick-up trucks serving as minibuses, called **"sǒrng tǎihw"**, **Túk-Túk** (motorized three-wheeled vehicles), **sǎrm lór** (non-motorized tricycle rickshaws), and last but not least, **mor-Ter-sai ráp jârng** (motorcycle taxis). They operate a taxi service and you can flag them down at any reasonable point. You must agree the fare before you get in, so be prepared to bargain. Some drivers may not speak English, so have your destination written down in Thai on a piece of paper.

▌ There are two types of taxis in Bangkok, – ordinary taxis and the so-called "taxi-meter". The "taxi-meter" is the latest attempt by the Thai authorities to force drivers to use meters for the convenience of the passengers. The meters installed in this type of taxi are designed to charge according to a combination of distance and time taken to travel. However, this system has met with limited success only, since some drivers only use their meters for short trips and still prefer to haggle for longer journeys.

Useful signs

ที่หยุดรถประจำทาง	têe yùt rót Pra-jam-tarng	bus stop
แท็กซี่มิเตอร์	táihk-sêe mí-têr	metered taxi
ห้ามสูบบุหรี่	hârm sòop bu-rèe	no smoking

Useful words

boat	reuar
bus	rót may
bus route	săi
conductor	gra-Păo
driver	kon kàp
inspector	nai Trùat

Public buses and riverbuses

Where is the bus stop?	Pâi rót may Pai tarng nǎi
Where do I catch the bus for …?	rót may Pai … kêuhn têe nǎi
Where do I catch the boat for …?	reuar Pai … kêuhn têe nǎi
Which bus/boat goes to …?	rót may/reuar sǎi nǎi Pai …
Is this the bus/boat for …?	rót may/reuar sǎi nêe Pai … châi mái
One (for …), please	(Pai …) néuhng kon kráp/kâ
Two (for …), please	(Pai …) sǒrng kon kráp/kâ
Can you tell me where to get off?	têuhng láirw chûay bòrk dûay
Can you tell me when we get to …?	têuhng … láirw chûay bòrk dûay
Next stop, please	jòrt Pâi nâr dûay

Taxis, tuk-tuks etc.

How much is it to go to …?	Pai … tâo rài
… this address	… têe yòo née …
… the airport	… sa-nǎrm bin …
… the bus station	… sa-tǎr-nee kǒn-sòng …
… the railway station	… sa-tǎr-nee rót fai …
Too expensive	pairng Pai
Will you go for … baht?	… bàrt Pai mái
Let's go for … baht	… bàrt gôr láirw gan
Use the meter, please	chûay chái mí-têr dûay
Stop here/ there, please	jòrt Trong née/nán
Turn left	líaw sái
Turn right	líaw kwǎr
Straight on	Trong Pai
How much?	tâo-rài

| But we agreed on … baht | Tòk-long gan … bàrt nêe |
| Keep the change | mâi Tôrng torn |

You may hear

Public buses and riverbuses

Pai tarng nán	That way
yòo nân ngai	It's over there
săi sìp-hâr	It's route number 15
long Pâi nâr	Get off at the next stop

Taxis, tuk-tuks etc.

rót Tìt (mârk)	The traffic is (very) heavy
Tôrng kŏr pêrm nòy	I'll have to ask for more
mí-têr sĭa	The meter is out of order

Transport hire

▌This chapter deals with hiring cars, motorcycles, bicycles or boats for private transport.

▌You drive on the left in Thailand and you must have an international driving licence. Although few tourists hire a car to drive by themselves, many hire motorcycles for sightseeing while they stay at resorts and in some cities.

▌Remember that Thai motorists are seldom insured, so if you have an accident you may have to negotiate with the other party or parties involved about responsibility and payment for damage. The police are called in if an agreement cannot be reached or if there are any injuries or deaths.

▌Road distance in Thailand is measured in kilometres. International road signs are used on roads and highways, although in some places, you may see road signs in Thai only.

Useful signs

Road signs

ทางหลวงแผ่นดิน	tarng lŭang pàirn-din	state highways
60 ก.ม.	hòk-sìp gi-loh	60 kilometres
2 ม.	sŏrng máyt	2 metres
10 ตัน	sìp Tan	10 tons
อันตราย	an-Ta-rai	danger
ระวัง	rá-wang	caution
ทางโค้ง	tarng kóhng	bend
ทางเบี่ยง	tarng bìang	diversion
ขับช้า ๆ	kàp chár-chár	drive slowly

ชิดซ้าย	chít sái	keep to the left
หยุด	yùt	stop/halt
หยุดตรวจ	yùt Trùat	checkpoint
รถเดินทางเดียว	rót dern tarng diaw	one-way street
ห้ามรถทุกชนิด	hârm rót túk cha-nít	no vehicles
ห้ามเข้า	hârm kâo	no entry
ห้ามแซง	hârm sairng	no overtaking
ห้ามจอด	hârm jòrt	no parking
ห้ามหยุด	hârm yùt	no stopping
ห้ามเลี้ยว	hârm líaw	no turning
ห้ามกลับรถ	hârm glàp rót	no U-turns
เขตชุมชน	kàyt chum-chon	built-up area
ลดความเร็ว	lót kwarm rehw	reduce speed
โรงพยาบาล ห้ามใช้เสียง	rohng pa-yar-barn : hârm chái sĭang	hospital : do not sound your horn
โรงเรียน	rohng rian	school
ทางรถไฟ	tarng rót fai	railway

Petrol stations and garages

อู่	òo	garage
บริการ 24 ช.ม.	bor-ri-garn yêe-sìp-sèe chûa-mohng	24-hour service
บริการซ่อมรถ	bor-ri-garn sôrm rót	repairs
อะไหล่	a-lài	spares
ปะยาง	Pà yarng	punctures repaired
ห้ามสูบบุหรี่	hârm sòop bu-rèe	no smoking
ดีเซล	dee-sayn	diesel
เบนซิน	bayn-sin	petrol/gasoline
ซุปเปอร์	súp-pêr	super
ธรรมดา	tam-ma-dar	regular
ไร้สารตะกั่ว	rái sărn Ta-gùa	unleaded

Hiring and driving

I want to hire …	pǒm/di-chán kǒr châo …
… a bicycle	… jàk-gra-yarn
… a boat	… reuar
… a car	… rót
… a motorcycle	… mor-Ter-sai
… a van	… rót Tôo
with a chauffeur	prórm kon kàp
How much is it …?	… tâo-rài
… per hour	chûa-mohng lá …
… per day	wan lá …
… per week	ar-tít lá …
Is there a charge per kilometre?	kít kâr chǎo Pehn gi-loh dûay mái
Where shall I return the car to?	Tôrng keurn rót têe nǎi
Here's my driving licence	nêe bai kàp-kèe
Where can I park?	jà jòrt dâi têe nǎi
Can I park here?	jòrt têe nêe dâi mái

Petrol stations

Where's the (nearest) petrol station?	Pám nám-man (glâi têe sùt) Pai tarng nǎi
Fill her up, please	Term Tehm tǎng
10 litres of 4 star, please	Term sèe dao sìp lít
500 baht of regular, please	Term tam-ma-dar hâr róy bàrt
I'd like some …	chûay Term … dûay
… oil	… nám-man krêuarng …
… water	… nárm …
Would you check the tyres, please?	chûay doo yarng dûay

66

Would you put some air in ..., please?	chûay Term lom ... dûay
... the front tyre/tyres ...	... yarng nâr ...
... the rear tyre/tyres ...	... yarng lăng ...
... the front left tyre ...	... yarng lór nâr sái ...
... the front right tyre ...	... yarng lór nâr kwăr ...
... the rear left tyre ...	... yarng lór lăng sái ...
... the rear right tyre ...	... yarng lór lăng kwăr ...

Garages

Where's the nearest garage?	òo glâi têe sùt Pai tarng năi
Do you do repairs here?	Sôrm rót dâi mái
Would you check ..., please?	chûay doo ... dûay
Can you repair ...?	sôrm ... dâi mái
... the brake ...	... bràyk ...
... the clutch ...	... klát ...
... the engine ...	... krêuarng ...
... the exhaust pipe ...	... tôr ai-sĭa ...
... the gear/transmission ...	... gia ...
... the shock absorber ...	... chóhk-âp ...
The engine is overheating	krêuarng rórn
How long will it take?	chái way-lar narn mái

Chartering

I'd like to charter ... to ...	kŏr măo ... Pai ...
... the boat ...	... reuar ...
... the car ...	... rót ...
... the van ...	... rót Tôo ...
How much is it ...?	... tâo-rài
... per hour	chûa-mohng lá ...
... per day	wan lá ...
... per half-day	krêuhng wan ...

Can you pick me up at my hotel? | Pai ráp tée rohng-rairm dâi mái
I'll meet you here | jer gan tée nêe
We'll meet you at the jetty | jer gan tée târ reuar
Could you let me/us off at …? | Pai sòng tée … dûay
… the station | … sa-tár-nee …
… that jetty | … târ reuar nán …

You may hear

Hiring and driving

Tôrng warng ngern mát-jam | I'll need a deposit
kŏr doo bai kàp-kèe dûay | Your driving licence, please
Tôrng keurn rót tée nêe | You'll have to return the car here
Tôrng keurn nám-man Tehm tăng | You must return it with a full tank

Petrol stations

Term tâo rài kráp/ká | How much petrol would you like?
súp-per rĕur tam-ma-dar | Super or regular?
yarng òrn | You have a flat tyre
Tôrng Term lom | It needs some air
tée Term lom yôo Trong nán | The air line is over there

Garages

Tôrng Plìan … | … needs changing
wan diaw mâi sèht | It can't be done in a day

At the beach

On most beaches, you should dress properly. Bathing nude on beaches in Thailand is illegal. Topless bathing for females may cause offence to Thais and is not a good idea, except on beaches which are exclusively for tourists. Despite their false reputation to the contrary, Thais are very modest in this respect.

Useful signs

หาดส่วนตัว	hàrt sùan-Tua	private beach
ห้ามเข้า	hârm kâo	no entry
อันตรายน้ำลึก	an-Ta-rai nárm léuhk	danger! deep water
ห้ามเล่นน้ำ	hârm lêhn nárm	no swimming
ที่อาบน้ำจืด	têe àrp nárm jèurt	freshwater shower

Useful words

beach	chai hàrt
seaside	chai ta-lay
to sunbathe	àrp dàirt

You may want to say

Can I swim here?	wâi nárm Trong née dâi mái
Is it dangerous … here?	… Trong née an-Ta-rai mái
… to swim …	wâi nárm …
… to scuba dive …	dam nárm …

69

... to dive (*head first*) ...	gra-dòht nárm ...
... to windsurf ...	win-sérp ...
Is it deep here?	nárm léuhk mái
Where can I hire ...?	jà châo ... dâi têe nǎi
... a beach umbrella	... rôm gan dàirt ...
... a deckchair	... gâo-êe chai hàrt ...
... a water scooter	... sa-góot-têr ...
How much is it ...?	... tâo-rài
... per hour	chûa-mohng lá ...
... per day	wan lá ...
I'm going to the beach	jà Pai chai hàrt
Are you coming for a swim?	wâi nárm mái
I can't ...	... mâi Pehn
... swim	wâi nárm ...
... scuba dive	dam nárm ...
Will you keep an eye on my things?	chûay doo kǒrng hâi nòy dâi mái
I have no ...	mâi mee ...
... bikini	... bee-gee-nêe
... sunglasses	... wâirn gan dàirt
... suntan lotion	... kreem tar àrp dàirt
... suntan oil	... nám-man tar àrp dàirt
... swimming costume	... chút wâi nárm/chút àrp nárm
... swimming trunks	... garng-gayng wâi nárm
... towel	... pâr chéht Tua

You may hear

châo chút dam nárm mái	Would you like to hire diving gear?
nûat mái	Would you like a massage?
Trong née an-Ta-rai	It's dangerous here

Accommodation

▌ Hotels in Thailand are not usually graded unless they are part of an international chain. Standards vary widely, from the luxury of Bangkok's Oriental Hotel to budget guest houses and bungalows. Mid-range hotels tend to offer both air-conditioned rooms and rooms with a fan, the latter being cheaper. If you prefer not to have a room with air-conditioning, you should make a point of asking for this, as it is often automatically assumed that foreign tourists will require this facility. Only the very cheapest guest houses have shared bathrooms and toilet facilities. Meals are not usually included as part of the hotel charge.

▌ Apart from hotels and guest houses, most Thai towns and cities have drive-in motels. Rooms here are available overnight but are usually let on an hourly basis. Bear in mind, though, that the locals normally use this type of motel for activities other than sleeping!

Useful Signs

โรงแรม	rohng-rairm	hotel
โอเต็ล	hoh-tehn	hotel
ห้องว่าง	hôrng wârng	vacancies/rooms to let
แผนกต้อนรับ	pa-nàirk Tôrn-ráp	reception
ทางออก	tarng òrk	exit
ทางออกฉุกเฉิน	tarng òrk chùk-chěrn	emergency exit
ทางหนีไฟ	tarng něe fai	fire exit
ห้องสุขา/ห้องน้ำ	hôrng sù-kǎr/hôrng nárm	toilets
ชาย/สุภาพบุรุษ	chai/sù-pârp bu-rùt	gentlemen
หญิง/สุภาพสตรี	yǐng/sù-pârp sàt-Tree	ladies

Useful Words

bath	àrng àrp-nárm
bed	Tiang
key	gun-jair
motel	rohng-rairm mârn-rôot
number	ber
room	hôrng

You may want to say

Do you have …?	mee … wârng mái
… a room	… hôrng …
… a single room	… hôrng dìaw …
… a double room	… hôrng kôo …
… with a shower	… hôrng mee fàk bua …
… with air-conditioning	… hôrng air …
… with a fan	… hôrng pát-lom …
Is the room en suite?	mee hôrng nárm nai Tua mái
I'll be staying for …	jà yòo …
… one night	… nèuhng keurn
… two nights	… sŏrng keurn
… one week	… nèuhng ar-tít
I don't know how long I'll be staying yet	yang mâi róo wâr jà yòo gèe keurn
How much is it (per night)?	(keurn lá) tâo-rài
Do you have anything cheaper?	mee tòok gwàr née mái
Is there another hotel nearby?	mee rohng-rairm èurn mái
I have a reservation	pŏm/di-chán jorng hôrng wái láirw
My name is …	pŏm/di-chán chêur …
Can I see the room first?	kŏr doo hôrng gòrn dâi mái

Which floor is the room on?	hôrng yòo chán nǎi
Can I leave something in the safe?	fàrk kǒrng wái nai sáyp dâi mái
Can I have a receipt?	kǒr bai ráp dûay kráp/kâ
Can I have my things from the safe?	kǒr kǒrng fàrk nai sáyp keurn dûay kráp/kâ
The key, please	kǒr gun-jair hôrng kráp/kâ
Room ..., please	hôrng ber ... kráp/kâ
(See Number Section)	
Are there any messages for me?	mee jòt-mǎi těurng pǒm/di-chán mái
Can I have ... please?	kǒr ... dâi mái
... (clean) sheets ...	... pâr Poo-têe-norn (sa-àrt) ...
... a blanket ...	... pâr hòm ...
... a pillow ...	... mǒrn ...
... a pillowcase ...	... Plòrk mǒrn ...
... a towel ...	... pâr chét Tua ...
... a bar of soap ...	... sa-bòo ...
I'm leaving tomorrow	pǒm/di-chán jà Pai prûng née
The bill, please	chûay kít ngern dûay
Do you take ...?	jài Pehn ... dâi mái
... credit cards	... bàt kray-dìt ...
... traveller's cheques	... chéhk dern tarng ...

You may hear

hôrng Tehm	We are full
jà yòo gèe keurn	For how many nights?
kun chêur a-rai	What's your name?
kǒr doo párt-sa-Pòrt	Your passport, please
chûay gròrk bàirp form dûay	Fill in the registration form, please
rao ráp Tàir ngern sòt	We only take cash

Telephones

▌ You can dial direct between the main cities in Thailand with little difficulty but in smaller towns you may have to go to the local telephone exchanges and make your calls from there.

▌ You can make international calls from government telephone offices, Bangkok GPO or from large hotels, but expect to pay a large surcharge if you call from a hotel.

▌ You can also make local telephone calls from public phone boxes, hotels and some shops.

▌ Although the Thai word for 'to telephone' is *"toh-ra-sàp"*, Thais often shorten this to *"toh"*, meaning 'to phone'.

▌ The Thai telephone directory lists subscribers' names by their first name, not by the family name. This includes directories in both Thai and English. Thus if you want to find the telephone number of a Mr Pisit Sakulthai, you should look for it under 'p' and not 's'.

▌ Some shops, especially in tourist areas, offer international telephone and/or fax services. You will see a sign displayed on the shop front.

Useful signs

(โทรศัพท์) เสีย	(toh-ra-sàp) sĭa	(Phone) out of order
โทรศัพท์ใช้บัตร	toh-ra-sàp chái bàt	cardphone
โทรศัพท์ทางไกล	toh-ra-sàp tarng glai	long-distance telephone
โทรสาร (แฟกส์)	toh-ra-sârn (fàihk)	facsimile (fax)

Useful words

area code	rá-hàt
coin	rĭan
extension	Tòr
international call	toh-ra-sàp Tàrng Pra-tâyt
national long-distance call	toh-ra-sàp tarng glai nai Pra-tâyt
number	măi-lâyk *or* ber
phonecard	bàt toh-ra-sàp
telephone	toh-ra-sàp
telephone box	Tôo toh-ra-sàp
telephone directory	sa-mùt toh-ra-sàp

You may want to say

Is there a phone around here?	tăihw née mee toh-ra-sàp mái
Can I …?	kŏr … dâi mái
… use your phone	… chái toh-ra-sàp …
… have some one-baht coins	… lâirk rĭan bàrt …
What coins do I need?	chái rĭan a-rai kráp/ká
Do you have a telephone directory?	mee sa-mùt toh-ra-sàp mái kráp/ká
I want to call …	pŏm/di-chán jà toh Pai …
… England	… ang-grìt
… Germany	… yer-ra-man
What's the charge for calling …?	kâr toh Pai … tâo-rài
… the USA	… a-may-rí-gar …
… France	… fa-ràng-sàyt …
I want to reverse the charges	kŏr gèhp ngern Plai tarng
The number is …	toh-ra-sàp măi-lâyk …
Extension (number) …	Tòr ber …

It's …(caller)… speaking	(…) pôot sǎi kráp/kâ
Do you speak English?	kun pôot ang-grìt dâi mái
Can I speak to …?	kǒr pôot gàp … kráp/kâ
Slowly, please	pôot chár-chár kráp/kâ
Could you repeat that?	chûay pôot sám dâi mái
When will he/she be back?	káo jà glàp mar mêuar rài
Can I leave a message for him/her?	fàrk bòrk káo nòy dâi mái
Tell him/her that … called	bòrk káo wâr … toh mar
I'll call again/back later	pǒm/di-chán jà toh mar èek
I've been cut off	sǎi kàrt
It's a bad line	sǎi mâi dee
The line's engaged	sǎi mâi wârng
There's no answer	mâi mee kon ráp sǎi
Could you try again?	chûay Tòr mài dâi mái
How much is the charge?	kâr toh tâo-rài

You may hear

krai pôot kráp/ká	Who's calling?
ror dǐaw kráp/kâ	One moment, please
pǒm/di-chán jà ohn sǎi Pai hâi	I'm putting you through
sǎi mâi wârng	The line's engaged
kun jà ror mái	Do you want to hold?
káo mâi yòo/káo òrk Pai kârng nôrk	He/She is not in
toh mar mài ná kráp/ká	Please try again later
mâi mee kon ráp sǎi	There's no answer
kun Tòr pìt	You've got the wrong number
têe nêe kon chêur nán	There's no person of that name here

Post office

▌ Thailand has a very efficient postal service. Bangkok's central post office (GPO) on Charoen Krung Road (called New Road on some maps) is open from 8 a.m. to 8 p.m. Monday to Friday and from 9 a.m. to 1 p.m. weekends and public holidays. The GPO also provides a telephone and telegram service 24 hours a day.

▌ There is also an efficiently-run poste restante service in operation at the GPO. If you are planning on a long stay in Thailand, you can arrange for friends and relatives to send letters to you there.

▌ Other main post offices in Bangkok and the other major cities close at 6 p.m. on weekdays and are open until lunchtime on Saturdays.

▌ As in other countries, sending cash by post is not recommended.

Useful signs

ไปรษณียากร	Prai-sa-nee-yar-gorn	stamps
โทรเลข	toh-ra-lâyk	telegram
โทรศัพท์ (ระหว่างประเทศ)	toh-ra-sàp (rá-wàrng Pra-tâyt)	(international) telephone
โทรสารสาธารณะ	toh-ra-sărn săr-tar-ra-ná	fax service
พัสดุไปรษณีย์	pát-sa-dù Prai-sa-nee	parcels
ไปรษณีย์ด่วนพิเศษ EMS	Prai-sa-nee dùan pí-sàyt	special delivery service
ลงทะเบียน	long ta-bian	registered mail
ธนาณัติ	ta-nar-nát	postal order
ให้บริการชั้นบน	hâi bor-ri-garn chán bon	service upstairs
กรุงเทพฯ	grung-tâyp	Bangkok
ที่อื่น ๆ	têe èurn-èurn	other places

Useful words

address	têe-yòo
letter	jòt-măi
post office	Prai-sa-nee
postcode	rá-hàt Prai-sa-nee
recipient	pôo ráp
sender	pôo sòng
stamp	sa-Taihm

You may want to say

How long does it take to get to .... ?	sòng jòt-măi Pai ..... gèe wan tĕuhng
I want to send this letter by ...	jòt-măi née jà sòng Pai ...
... airmail	... tarng ar-gàrt
... surface mail	... tarng reuar
... registered mail	... bàirp long ta-bian
... express mail	... bàirp dùan
... EMS (special delivery service)	... bàirp ee-ehm-áyt
How much is a letter to England?	kâr sòng jòt-măi Pai ang-grìt tâo-rài
An aerogramme, please	kŏr air-roh-grairm nèuhng bai
Two stamps for postcards to the USA, please	kŏr sa-Taihm sŏrng duang sòng Póht-sa-gárt Pai a-may-rí-gar
Where can I post this?	nêe sòng dâi têe năi
Where is the letterbox?	Tôo Prai-sa-nee yòo têe năi
It's a present, of no commercial value	nêe Pehn kŏrng-kwăn mâi mee kâr a-rai
I want to send a telegram to	pŏm/di-chán kŏr sòng toh-ra-lâyk Pai .....

78

Tôrng-garn (sa-Taihm) gèe duang	How many (stamps) do you want?
sòng Pai năi	Where to?
a-rai yòo nai hòr	What is in the parcel?
chûay gròrk bàirp form dûay	Please fill in this form
kĭan kôr kwarm sòng toh-ra-lâyk nai form née	Write your telegram message on this form
táng mòt ... bàrt	That'll be ... baht

Banks and changing money

▌ Banks are open from 8.30 a.m. to 3.30 p.m. on weekdays. In Bangkok and the other major cities, many banks also operate currency exchange booths outside their own buildings or in tourist areas. These booths are often open until 7 or 8 p.m., seven days a week.

▌ Banks charge a fixed commission and duty stamps for each traveller's cheque cashed, regardless of the denomination, so you will save on commission if you take larger cheque denominations.

Useful signs

ธนาคาร	ta-nar-karn	bank
รับแลกเงิน	ráp lâirk ngern	exchange/bureau de change
เปิด	Pèrt	open
ปิด	Pìt	closed

Useful words

bank charges/commission	kâr tam-niam
banknote	ta-na-bàt or báihng
cash	ngern sòt
coin	rĭan
credit card	bàt kray-dìt
duty stamp	kâr ar-gorn
exchange rate	àt-Trar lâirk-Plìan
money	ngern
small change	sàyt sa-Tarng

traveller's cheque	chéhk dern tarng
baht	bàrt *or* ngern bàrt
French franc	ngern frang fa-ràng-sàyt
German mark	ngern márk yer-ra-man
pound sterling	ngern Porn ang-grìt
US dollar	ngern don-lâr sa-hà-rát

You may want to say

I'd like to …	pŏm/di-chán kŏr …
… cash some traveller's cheques	… lâirk chéhk dern tarng
… change this into baht	… lâirk Pehn ngern bàrt
… use my credit card to get some cash	… chái bàt kray-dìt bèrk ngern sòt
What's the exchange rate?	àt-Trar lâirk-Plìan tâo-rài
What's the commission?	kâr tam-niam tâo-rài
Can I have something smaller?	kŏr báihng yôy dâi mái

You may hear

kŏr párt-sa-Pòrt dûay	Your passport, please
chûay sehn chêur Trong née	Sign here, please
rao mâi ráp lâirk ngern sa-gun …	We don't exchange … (currency)
rao mâi mee bor-ri-garn lâirk ngern	We have no exchange service

Eating and drinking

▌ There are many places where you can eat and drink in Thailand, ranging from expensive restaurants to the numerous food stalls. Restaurants generally serve Thai food, but some large restaurants serve Chinese or Western food as well. There are also quite a few international restaurants, particularly in Bangkok.

▌ There are two words in Thai for restaurant; *rárn ar-hǎrn* and *pát-Tar-karn*. The former is by far the most common and covers anything from a cheap noodle shop to a more expensive establishment. The word **pát-Tar-karn** is reserved for the top end of the market – the largest and most expensive eating places.

▌ A typical Thai meal consists of plain boiled rice accompanied by several kinds of dishes, for example a curry dish, a soup dish, a stir-fried dish, a deep-fried or grilled dish and a spicy salad dish. You don't have to order all of them, but if you order a hot (spicy) dish, it is a good idea to order a non-spicy one as well, to complement the taste. The dishes are served and eaten at the same time and are shared among the group of diners. Unlike what you may have experienced in Thai restaurants abroad, a Thai meal does not come in separate courses. However, a dessert is normally served at the end of the main meal, although not all restaurants or food stalls have a dessert menu.

▌ If you are on your own, you may order just one or two dishes in a restaurant. A cheaper alternative is to have a meal in a small restaurant, a *"rárn kâo gairng"*, which serves a variety of prepared dishes on display at the front counter. You can order dishes served on rice – *'rârt kâo'* (literally 'over rice').

▌ If you prefer noodles to rice, there are many types of noodle restaurants and noodle stalls to choose from. Typical noodle restaurants and stalls specialize in one kind of meat, e.g. pork noodle restaurants, beef and meatball noodle restaurants, fish ball noodle restaurants or stir-fried noodle restaurants. Only in large restaurants which serve a variety of foods will there be several types of meat on the noodle menu. When you have decided what to order, you will also have to specify what kind of noodles you require. (See Menu Reader)

▍ Thai food is usually eaten with a fork and spoon. If you haven't tried yet, you will find it is a lot easier to eat rice with a spoon than with a fork. For a noodles dish, chopsticks are usually used.

▍ Most restaurants in Thailand serve alcohol and soft drinks. Many also serve other kinds of drinks, such as coffee and tea. Food stalls do not normally serve drinks, but they can order some for you from nearby drink stalls.

▍ Most alcoholic drinks are locally-produced, but some beers are international brands, brewed in Thailand under licence. Foreign whiskies, such as Scotch, are served only in large restaurants or bars and nightclubs.

▍ The Thai word for 'to eat' is *'gin'* and you will hear people use this word in everyday conversation. Among business colleagues, or when you are talking to elders or people of superior status, you should use a polite version of the word, which is *'tarn'*. Both words are used here and they are interchangeable, except in terms of formality as explained above.

▍ When you want to order or ask for something, just use the word *'kŏr'* which means "Can I have …", followed by whatever you want to order.

▍ For buying fruits and vegetables in the local markets, the common word for '100 grams' is *"kèet"*. So if you want to buy something for 100 grams, just say "one **kèet** of …"; 200 grams is "two **kèet** of …" and so on. (See also Conversion Tables section).

Useful signs

รายการอาหาร	rai-garn ar-hǎrn	menu
รายการเครื่องดื่ม	krêuarng-dèurm	drinks menu
ใหญ่	yài	large (size of dish)

ใหญ่พิเศษ	yài pí-sàyt	extra large
กลาง	glarng	medium
เล็ก	léhk	small
ธรรมดา	tam-ma-dar	normal
พิเศษ	pí-sàyt	special
ห้องน้ำ	hôrng nárm	toilets

Useful words

all-night food market	Ta-làrt Tôh-rûng
restaurant	rárn ar-hǎrn *or* pát-Tar-karn
Chinese ...	... jeen
Muslim ...	... ìt-sa-larm
vegetarian ...	... jay
noodle restaurant/stall	rárn gǔay-Tǐaw
on/'over' rice	rârt kâo
seafood	ar-hǎrn ta-lay
ashtray	têe kìa bu-rèe
bottle	kùat
bowl	charm
chair	gâo-êe
chopsticks	Ta-gìap
cup	tûay
fork	sôrm
glass	gâirw
knife	mêet
matches	mái-kèet
paper napkins	gra-dàrt tít-shôo
plate	jarn
spoon	chórn

table	Tó
teaspoon	chórn char
toothpick	mái jĭm fan

You may want to say

General phrases

I'm hungry	(pŏm/di-chán) hĭw
I'm thirsty	(pŏm/di-chán) hĭw nárm
Can you recommend a good restaurant?	rárn ar-hărn năi dee kráp/ká
I can eat ...	pŏm/di-chán tarn ... Pehn
I can't eat ...	pŏm/di-chán tarn ... mâi Pehn
... Thai food	... ar-hărn tai ...
... hot (spicy) food	... pèht ...
I like hot (spicy) food	pŏm/di-chán chôrp tarn pèht
I am a vegetarian	pŏm/di-chán gin jay
I don't eat ...	pŏm/di-chán mâi gin ...
... meat (all kinds)	... néuar sàt
... beef	... néuar (wua)
... pork	... mŏo
... vegetables	... pàk
I don't drink (alcohol)	pŏm/di-chán mâi dèurm lâo
Can I have ...?	kŏr ...
... a beer	... bia
... a Coke	... koh-lâr
For me	kŏrng pŏm
For him/her/them	kŏrng káo
Do you have ...?	mee ... mái
More ..., please	kŏr ... pêrm dûay

... rice ...	... kâo ...
... ice ...	... nárm-kǎihng ...
Where are the toilets?	hôrng nárm yòo têe nǎi
The bill, please	kít ngern dûay
Keep the change	mâi Tôrng torn

In eating and drinking places

A table for ..., please	... kráp/kâ
... one ...	têe diaw ...
... two ...	sǒrng têe ...
... three ...	sǎrm têe ...
Waiter/waitress	kun kráp/ká
The menu, please	kǒr may-noo dûay
What's this?	nêe a-rai
Is it (very) hot?	pèht (mârk) mái
What do you recommend?	kun wâr yàrng nǎi dee
Do you have any vegetarian dishes?	mee ar-hǎrn jay mái
Do you have any bottled water?	mee nárm kùat mái
I'll take this	ao an née
That's all	kâir née por
Excuse me, where is my order?	tó née yang mâi dâi ar-hǎrn
What's this?	nêe a-rai
I didn't order this	an née mâi dâi sàng
I ordered the chicken	pǒm/di-chán sàng gài
This isn't cooked	an née tam mâi sùk
One iced tea, please	kǒr char yehn nèuhng gâirw
A bottle of beer, please	kǒr bia nèuhng kùat
It's (very) good/delicious	a-ròy (mârk)

At take-away food, drink and fruit stalls

What's this?	nêe a-rai
How much is it/are they?	tâo-rài
… per kilogram	gi-loh lá …
… per 100 grams	kèet lá …
… per piece	an lá …
Two, please	ao sŏrng an
Half a kilo, please	ao krêuhng gi-loh
Three hundred grams, please	ao sărm kèet
(A bit) more, please	ao èek (nòy)
A bit less, please	ao òrk nòy
That's enough	por láirw
How much is that?	táng mòt tâo-rài
My change, please	kŏr ngern torn dûay

You may hear

Sitting down

chern kráp/kâ	Welcome
gèe têe kráp/ká	How many are there of you?
chern nâng kráp/kâ	Take a seat, please
Tó née jorng láirw	This table is already reserved
chern Tó nán kráp/kâ	Take that table, please

Giving one's orders

sàng a-rai kráp/ká	What would you like to order?
sàng láirw rĕur yang	Have you ordered yet?

an née …	This is …
… (mâi) dee	… (not) good
… (mâi) pèht	… (not) hot *(spicy)*
gin pèht dâi mái	Can you eat hot (spicy) food?
yài rĕur léhk	Large or small?
tam-ma-dar rĕur pí-sàyt	Normal or special?
an năi	Which one?
an née mâi mee	We have run out of it
sàng a-rai èek mái	Anything else?
ao tâo-rài	How much/many would you like?
ao gèe kùat	How many bottles would you like?
ráp nárm a-rai	Anything to drink?

In this book, we categorize the dishes not according to the type of meat used but the way they have been cooked, for example, soups and curries, stir-fried dishes, grilled dishes and so on. We have also included an extra section for foods which you may find at take-away food stalls, which you can buy as a snack while sightseeing.

Rice – kâo – ข้าว

plain boiled rice	kâo sǔay	ข้าวสวย
rice soup	kâo Tôm	ข้าวต้ม
sticky rice	kâo nǐaw	ข้าวเหนียว

Basic meat and poultry

beef	néuar	เนื้อ
chicken	gài	ไก่
duck	Pèht	เป็ด
pork	mǒo	หมู

Basic seafoods

crab	Poo	ปู
fish	Plar	ปลา
prawn, shrimp	gûng	กุ้ง
shellfish	hǒy	หอย
squid	Plar-mèuhk	ปลาหมึก

Egg dishes – kài – ไข่

boiled egg	kài Tôm	ไข่ต้ม
fried egg	kài dao	ไข่ดาว
Thai-style omelette	kài jiaw	ไข่เจียว
… with minced pork	… mŏo sàp	… หมูสับ
omelette stuffed with minced pork and sliced tomatoes	kài yát sâi	ไข่ยัดไส้

Western food – อาหารฝรั่ง

bacon	bay-kôn	เบคอน
bread	ka-nŏm Pang	ขนมปัง
butter	noei	เนย
ham	mŏo-haihm	หมูแฮม
jam	yairm	แยม
sausages	sâi-gròrk	ไส้กรอก
steak	sa-Táyk	สะเต็ก

Soups and curries – gairng jèurt and gairng pèht แกงจืดและแกงเผ็ด

coconut soup with chicken	Tôm kàr gài	ต้มข่าไก่
green curry	gairng kĭaw wărn	แกงเขียวหวาน
red curry	gairng pèht	แกงเผ็ด
… with beef	… néuar	… เนื้อ
… with chicken	… gài	… ไก่
… with prawn	… gûng	… กุ้ง
… with roast duck	… Pèht yârng	… เป็ดย่าง

hot and sour seafood soup	Pó-Tàirk	โป๊ะแตก
hot and sour soup	Tôm yam	ต้มยำ
… with chicken	… gài	ไก่
… with prawns	… gûng	กุ้ง
Indian-style mild curry	gairng ga-rèe	แกงกะหรี่
… with beef	… néuar	เนื้อ
… with chicken	… gài	ไก่
pork and vegetable soup	gairng jèurt	แกงจืด
… with beancurd	… Tâo-hôo	เต้าหู้
… with fish balls	… lôok-chín (Plar)	ลูกชิ้น (ปลา)
rich, spicy curry	gairng mát-sa-màn	แกงมัสมั่น
… with beef	… néuar	เนื้อ
… with chicken	… gài	ไก่
spicy beef curry without coconut milk	gairng Pàr néuar	แกงป่าเนื้อ
spicy tamarind soup	gairng sôm	แกงส้ม
steamed curried fish	hòr-mòk Plar	ห่อหมกปลา
thick peanut curry	pa-nairng	พะแนง
… with beef	… néuar	เนื้อ
… with chicken	… gài	ไก่

Stir-fried dishes – pàt – อาหารผัด

beef in oyster sauce	pàt néuar nám-man hòy	ผัดเนื้อน้ำมันหอย
chicken with bamboo shoots	gài pàt nòr-mái	ไก่ผัดหน่อไม้
chicken with cashew nuts	gài pàt ma-mûang hĭm-ma-parn	ไก่ผัดมะม่วงหิมพานต์
chillies	pàt prík	ผัดพริก
chillies and basil	pàt ga-prao	ผัดกะเพรา
… with beef	… néuar	เนื้อ
… with chicken	… gài	ไก่

... with pork	... mŏo	หมู
garlic and pepper	pàt gra-tiam prík-tai	ผัดกระเทียมพริกไทย
... with pork	... mŏo	หมู
... with prawns	... gûng	กุ้ง
... with squid	... Plar-mèuhk	ปลาหมึก
ginger	pàt kĭng	ผัดขิง
... with chicken	... gài	ไก่
... with pork	... mŏo	หมู
stir-fried beansprouts in oyster sauce	pàt tùa-ngôrk	ผัดถั่วงอก
stir-fried Chinese spinach in bean sauce	pàt pàk-bûng	ผัดผักบุ้ง
stir-fried green cabbage	pàt ka-nár	ผัดคะน้า
... with crispy pork	... mŏo gròrp	หมูกรอบ
... with salted fish	... Plar-kehm	ปลาเค็ม
... in oyster sauce	... nám-man hŏy	น้ำมันหอย
stir-fried mixed vegetables	pàt pàk	ผัดผัก
sweet and sour	pàt Prîaw-wărn	ผัดเปรี้ยวหวาน
... with pork	... mŏo	หมู
... with prawns	... gûng	กุ้ง

Deep-fried dishes – tôrt – อาหารทอด

chicken in batter	gài tôrt	ไก่ทอด
crisp-fried fish	Plar tôrt	ปลาทอด
prawns in batter	gûng tôrt	กุ้งทอด
spicy fish cakes	tôrt-man	ทอดมัน

Grilled dishes – yârng – อาหารย่าง

barbecued chicken	gài yârng	ไก่ย่าง
barbecued pork	mŏo yârng	หมูย่าง
charcoal-grilled beef	néuar yârng	เนื้อย่าง
charcoal-grilled fish	Plar păo	ปลาเผา
charcoal-grilled prawns	gûng păo	กุ้งเผา
roast duck	Pèht yârng	เป็ดย่าง

Spicy salad dishes – yam – อาหารยำ

yam is a cold, savoury dish with a basic ingredient such as squid, prawns or beef marinaded in a piquant dressing. The ingredients for this dressing include fresh chilli, red onion, garlic, lemon grass, lime leaves, fish sauce and lime juice.

spicy charcoal-grilled beef with ground roasted rice	(néuar) nárm-Tòk	(เนื้อ) น้ำตก
spicy green papaya salad	sôm-Tam	ส้มตำ
spicy salad	yam	ยำ
… with beef	… néuar	เนื้อ
… with glass noodles	… wún-sêhn	วุ้นเส้น
… with squid	… Plar-mèuhk	ปลาหมึก
spicy salad mixed with ground roasted rice	lârp	ลาบ
… with chicken	… gài	ไก่
… with pork	… mŏo	หมู
… with minced beef	… néuar	เนื้อ

One-dish meals - อาหารจานเดียว

American fried rice (fried with tomato ketchup)	kâo pàt a-may-rí-gan	ข้าวผัดอเมริกัน
barbecued pork with rice	kâo mŏo dairng	ข้าวหมูแดง
casseroled pork loin with rice	kâo kăr mŏo	ข้าวขาหมู
chicken/pork rice gruel	jóhk gài/mŏo (sài kài)	โจ๊กไก่/ หมู
chicken/fish/pork/ prawn rice soup	kâo Tôm gài/Plar/ mŏo/gûng	ข้าวต้มไก่/ ปลา/ หมู/ กุ้ง
fried rice (with egg)	kâo pàt (sài kài)	ข้าวผัด (ใส่ไข่)
Muslim-style chicken with saffron rice	kâo mòk gài	ข้าวหมกไก่
northern-style noodles with beef or chicken curry	kâo soy	ข้าวซอย
roast duck with rice	kâo nâr Pèht	ข้าวหน้าเป็ด
steamed chicken and rice cooked in chicken stock	kâo man gài	ข้าวมันไก่
stir-fried mussels in batter	hŏy tôrt	หอยทอด
white Thai noodles with curry	ka-nŏm jeen nárm-yar	ขนมจีนน้ำยา
northern-style noodles with beef or chicken curry	kâo soy	ข้าวซอย
roast duck with rice	kâo nâr Pèht	ข้าวหน้าเป็ด
steamed chicken and rice cooked in chicken stock	kâo man gài	ข้าวมันไก่
white Thai noodles with curry	ka-nŏm jeen nárm-yar	ขนมจีนน้ำยา

Noodle dishes – gŭay-Tĭaw – ก๋วยเตี๋ยว

Varieties of noodles

egg noodles	ba-mèe	บะหมี่
thick rice noodles	sêhn yài	เส้นใหญ่
thin rice noodles	sêhn léhk	เส้นเล็ก
vermicelli	sêhn mèe	เส้นหมี่

Types of meat served with noodles

beef	néuar	เนื้อ
chicken	gài	ไก่
duck	Pèht	เป็ด
fish balls	lôok-chín Plar	ลูกชิ้นปลา
meatballs	lôok-chín néuar	ลูกชิ้นเนื้อ
pork	mŏo	หมู
pork balls	lôok-chín mŏo	ลูกชิ้นหมู

How noodles are served

with soup	nárm	น้ำ
with hot and sour soup	Tôm yam	ต้มยำ
without soup	hâirng	แห้ง
without beansprouts	mâi sài tùa ngôrk	ไม่ใส่ถั่วงอก
stir-fried in gravy	rârt nâr	ราดหน้า
stir-fried with dark soy sauce	pàt see-íw	ผัดซีอิ๊ว
thin rice noodles stir-fried with tofu, egg, peanuts and beansprouts	pàt tai	ผัดไทย

Condiments – krêurng Prung – เครื่องปรุง

chilli (in general)	prík	พริก
small, very hot chilli	prík kêe-nŏo	พริกขี้หนู
ground dried chilli	prík Pòn	พริกป่น

95

fish sauce	nám-Plar	น้ำปลา
chillies in fish sauce	nám-Plar prík	น้ำปลาพริก
lime	ma-nao	มะนาว
pepper	prík tai	พริกไทย
salt	gleuar	เกลือ
vinegar	nám-sôm săi-choo	น้ำส้มสายชู
chillies in vinegar	prík nám-sôm	พริกน้ำส้ม

Miscellaneous snacks available at food stalls

barbecued fresh squid	Plar-mèuhk Pîng	ปลาหมึกปิ้ง
barbecued meat or fish balls	lôok-chín Pîng	ลูกชิ้นปิ้ง
beef/chicken/pork satay	néuar/gài/mŏo sa-Téh	เนื้อ/ไก่/หมู สะเต๊ะ
boiled corn on the cob	kâo-pôht Tôm	ข้าวโพดต้ม
charcoal-grilled corn on the cob	kâo-pôht Pîng	ข้าวโพดปิ้ง
charcoal-grilled dried squid	Plar-mèuhk yârng	ปลาหมึกย่าง
charcoal-grilled sticky rice with banana or taro root filling	kâo nĭaw Pîng	ข้าวเหนียวปิ้ง
deep-fried banana in batter	glûay kàirk	กล้วยแขก
deep-fried meat or fish balls	lôok-chín tôrt	ลูกชิ้นทอด
deep-fried north-eastern-style sausages	sâi-gròrk tôrt	ไส้กรอกทอด
deep-fried spring rolls	Por-Pía tôrt	ปอเปี๊ยะทอด
deep-fried tofu	Tâo-hôo tôrt	เต้าหู้ทอด
deep-fried wantons	gíaw tôrt	เกี๊ยวทอด
fresh spring rolls with tamarind sauce topping	Por-Pía sòt	ปอเปี๊ยะสด
grilled banana with coconut syrup topping	glûay Pîng	กล้วยปิ้ง
grilled Thai sausages	sâi-gròrk Pîng	ไส้กรอกปิ้ง

pork dumplings	ka-nŏm jèep	ขนมจีบ
roti (*Indian-style pancake*)	roh-Tee	โรตี
shrimp and minced pork toast	ka-nŏm Pang nâr mŏo	ขนมปังหน้าหมู
steamed buns	sar-la-Pao	ซาละเปา
... with barbecued pork filling	... sâi mŏo dairng	ไส้หมูแดง
... with pork filling	... sâi mŏo	ไส้หมู
... with sweet black bean paste filling	... sâi tùa	ไส้ถั่ว
sticky rice cooked in coconut cream with ...	kâo nĭaw nâr ...	ข้าวเหนียวหน้า
... coconut custard topping	... săng-ka-yăr	สังขยา
... shrimp topping	... gûng	กุ้ง
tapioca balls with pork filling	săr-koo sâi mŏo	สาคูไส้หมู
Thai pancakes	ka-nŏm bêuarng	ขนมเบื้อง

Desserts – kŏrng wărn – ของหวาน

banana in coconut cream	glûay bùat chee	กล้วยบวดชี
coconut custard	săng-ka-yăr	สังขยา
coconut ice cream	ai-Tim ga-tí	ไอศครีมกะทิ
glass noodle-like dessert made from green bean flour in coconut syrup	sa-lìm	สลิ่ม
ground peanut custard	ka-nŏm môr gairng	ขนมหม้อแกง
milk jelly with fruit cocktail	Tâo-huay yehn	เต้าฮวยเย็น
mock pomegranate seeds in coconut syrup	táp-tim gròrp	ทับทิมกรอบ
steamed banana in syrup	glûay chêuarm	กล้วยเชื่อม
sticky rice cooked in coconut cream served with fresh mango	kâo nĭaw ma-mûang	ข้าวเหนียวมะม่วง

Fruit – pǒn-la-mái – ผลไม้

apple	áihp-pêrn	แอ๊ปเปิ้ล
banana	glûay	กล้วย
coconut	ma-práo	มะพร้าว
durian	tú-rian	ทุเรียน
grape	a-ngùn	องุ่น
guava	fa-ràng	ฝรั่ง
jackfruit	ka-nǔn	ขนุน
longan	lam-yai	ลำไย
lychee	lín-jèe	ลิ้นจี่
mango	ma-mûang	มะม่วง
orange	sôm	ส้ม
papaya	má-lá-gor	มะละกอ
pineapple	sàp-Pa-rót	สับปะรด
pomelo	sôm-oh	ส้มโอ
rambutan	ngó	เงาะ
water melon	Tairng-moh	แตงโม

Drinks – krêuarng dèurm – เครื่องดื่ม

beer	bia	เบียร์
coffee	gar-fair	กาแฟ
iced black coffee	oh-líang	โอเลี้ยง
coffee with milk	gar-fair sài nom	กาแฟใส่นม
iced coffee with condensed milk	gar-fair yehn	กาแฟเย็น
chrysanthemum tea	nárm géhk-huay	น้ำเก๊กฮวย
fruit juice	nárm pǒn-la-mái	น้ำผลไม้
coconut juice	nárm ma-práo	น้ำมะพร้าว

guava juice	nárm fa-ràng	น้ำฝรั่ง
lemon juice/lemonade	nárm ma-nao	น้ำมะนาว
orange juice	nárm sôm	น้ำส้ม
sugar cane juice	nárm ôy	น้ำอ้อย
sugar palm juice	nárm Tarn sòt	น้ำตาลสด
ice, ice cube	nárm kǎihng	น้ำแข็ง
iced water	nárm kǎihng Plào	น้ำแข็งเปล่า
milk (fresh milk)	nom, nom sòt	นม,นมสด
condensed milk	nom kôn	นมข้น
soft (fizzy) drinks	nárm àt-lom	น้ำอัดลม
bottled	kùat	ขวด
canned	gra-Pŏrng	กระป๋อง
spirits	lâo	เหล้า
brandy	ba-ràn-dee	บรั่นดี
red wine	wai dairng	ไวน์แดง
white wine	wai kǎo	ไวน์ขาว
whisky	wít-sa-gêe	วิสกี้
tea	char	ชา
Chinese tea	char jeen	ชาจีน
hot tea with milk	char rórn	ชาร้อน
iced tea with condensed milk	char yehn	ชาเย็น
iced tea with sugar	char dam yehn	ชาดำเย็น
water	nárm	น้ำ
soda water	nárm soh-dar	น้ำโซดา

Shopping

▌ There is a wide variety of shopping facilities in Thailand, including markets, pavement stalls, shops, big department stores and modern shopping plazas.

▌ Most department stores open from 9 or 10 a.m. to 7 or 8 p.m. Some large stores stay open until 10 p.m. All are open 7 days a week.

▌ The opening hours of family-owned shops vary but, in general, they are open from 8 or 9 a.m. to 7 or 8 p.m., 7 days a week. Generally speaking, shops and stores in Thailand do not close for lunch.

▌ The opening times of fresh food markets vary, with some opening all day, others only in the morning or afternoon – it's best to check with the locals. See "Eating and Drinking" for buying food and drink.

▌ Prices are fixed in department stores, but elsewhere you may haggle to get the price you think reasonable. All shops and stores will provide carrier bags as a matter of course.

▌ Shop signs in Thailand do not indicate what kinds of shops they are. What is displayed above the shop door is usually the name of the establishment. You will have to look for a particular shop yourself, or go in and ask whether they sell the goods you want.

▌ A note worth remembering – although credit cards are now more widely used in Thailand than ever, cash payment is still preferred by many shops and department stores, even though they may have signs stating that credit cards are welcome. Outside Bangkok and the big cities, you will need to pay by cash. If shops or department stores accept payment by credit card, they may add on a surcharge unless the cards are issued by banks or card-issuers based in Thailand. The a surcharge varies according to which card you use.

Useful signs

เปิด	Pèrt	open
ปิด	Pìt	closed
ทางเข้า	tarng kâo	entrance
ทางออก	tarng òrk	exit
ทางออกฉุกเฉิน	tarng òrk chùk-chěrn	emergency exit
ทางหนีไฟ	tarng něe fai	fire exit
ราคา	rar-kar	price
ราคาพิเศษ	rar-kar pí-sàyt	special offer
ลดพิเศษ	lót pí-sàyt	special reduction
ลดราคา	lót rar-kar	sale
ซื้อ 1แถม 1	séur nèuhng tǎirm nèuhng	buy 1, get 1 free
กรุณาอย่าแตะ	ga-rú-nar yàr Tàih	please do not touch
โปรดเรียกพนักงานขาย	Pròht n̂ak pa-nák-ngarn kǎi	please ask a shop assistant for help

You may want to say

Looking for shops

Where's the (nearest) …? … (glâi têe sùt) yòo têe nǎi

Is there a/an … around here? tǎihw née mee … mái

List of shops

antique shop	rárn airn-Tík	ร้านแอนติ๊ค
barber's (shop)	rárn Tàt pǒm	ร้านตัดผม
beauty salon	rárn sěrm-sǔay	ร้านเสริมสวย
bookshop	rárn nǎng-sěur	ร้านหนังสือ
camera shop	rárn tài rôop	ร้านถ่ายรูป

101

chemist's	rárn kǎi yar	ร้านขายยา
clothes shop	rárn kǎi sêuar	ร้านขายเสื้อ
cobbler's	rárn sôrm rorng-táo	ร้านซ่อมรองเท้า
department store	hârng sàp-pa-sǐn-kár	ห้างสรรพสินค้า
dry cleaner's	rárn sák hâirng	ร้านซักแห้ง
goldsmith's	rárn torng	ร้านทอง
grocery store/shop	rárn cham	ร้านชำ
jeweller's	rárn péht	ร้านเพชร
laundry	rárn sák rêet	ร้านซักรีด
market	Ta-làrt	ตลาด
optician's	rárn wâirn-Tar	ร้านแว่นตา
shoe shop	rárn rorng-táo	ร้านรองเท้า
silk shop	rárn pâr-mǎi	ร้านผ้าไหม
stationer's	rárn krêuarng kǐan	ร้านเครื่องเขียน
supermarket	súp-pêr mar-gèht	ซูเปอร์มาร์เก็ต
tailor's	rárn Tàt sêuar	ร้านตัดเสื้อ
watchmaker's	rárn nar-lí-gar	ร้านนาฬิกา

General phrases

Excuse me	kun kráp/ká
Where can I buy …?	… mee kǎi têe nǎi
Have you got …?	mee … kǎi mái
I'm just looking	kǒr dern doo gòrn
When do you open?	rárn Pèrt gèe mohng
When do you close?	rárn Pìt gèe mohng
What is this?	nêe a-rai
Nothing else, thank you	por láirw kòrp-kun
Can you gift-wrap it, please?	chûay hòr kǒrng kwǎn dûay
A carrier bag, please	kǒr tǔng dûay
One more carrier bag, please	kǒr tǔng èek bai dûay

Buying

(A) Bangkok Post, please	kŏr barng-gòrk póht (nèuhng cha-bàp)
A box of matches, please	kŏr mái-kèet nèuhng glòrng
Two rolls of film, please	kŏr feem sŏrng múan
Black and white/colour film for colour slides	kăo-dam/sĕe sa-lái sĕe
Can I look at it/them, please?	kŏr doo nòy
That one there	an nán
This one here	an née
The one in the window	an têe choh nâr rárn
Can you show me some more?	kŏr doo an èurn èek dâi mái
What size is it? *(for dress, shirt)*	sái a-rai
What size is it? *(for shoes)*	ber a-rai
Have you got size …?	mee ber/sái … mái
I am a size …	kŏrng pŏm/di-chán ber/sái …
Can I try it/them on?	kŏr lorng sài dâi mái
Is there a mirror?	mee gra-jòk mái
It's/They're too big	lŭam Pai
It's/They're too small	káp Pai
It's too long	yao Pai
It's too short	sân Pai
Have you got anything …?	mee an … née mái
… bigger/larger	… yài gwàr …
… smaller	… léhk gwàr …
… cheaper	… tòok gwàr …
Have you got it/them in other colours?	mee sĕe èurn èek mái
I'd like it in red	Tôrng garn sĕe dairng
dark/light (colour)	kêhm/òrn
dark red	sĕe dairng kêhm
light green	sĕe kĭaw òrn

103

I'll take the red one	ao an sěe dairng
Will it shrink?	hòt mái
Will the colour run?	sěe Tòk mái
What is it/are they made of?	tam dûay a-rai
Is it/Are they made of …?	tam dûay … rěur Plào
… cotton	… pâr fâi …
… glass	… gâirw …
… gold	… torng …
… leather	… năng …
… metal	… loh-hà …
… plastic	… plárt-sa-Tìk …
… silk	… pâr măi …
… silver	… ngern …
… teak	… mái sàk …
… wood	… mái …
Is it/Are they …?	… rěur Plào
… handmade	tam dûay meur …
… real	kŏrng táir …
I'll come back later	dĭaw glàp mar mài
I'll take this one	ao an née

List of colours

colour	sěe	สี
beige	sěe bàyt	สีเบจ
black	sěe dam	สีดำ
black and white	kăo-dam	ขาวดำ
blue	sěe nám-ngern	สีน้ำเงิน
navy-blue	sěe grom-ma-târ	สีกรมท่า
sky-blue	sěe fár	สีฟ้า
brown	sěe nám-Tarn	สีน้ำตาล
cream	sěe kreem, sěe kài gài	สีครีม สีไข่ไก่

crimson	sěe lêuart mǒo	สีเลือดหมู
gold	sěe torng	สีทอง
green	sěe kǐaw	สีเขียว
grey	sěe tao	สีเทา
khaki	sěe gar-gee	สีกากี
orange	sěe sôm, sěe sàirt	สีส้ม สีแสด
pink	sěe chom-poo	สีชมพู
purple	sěe mûang	สีม่วง
red	sěe dairng	สีแดง
silver	sěe ngern	สีเงิน
violet	sěe mûang	สีม่วง
white	sěe kǎo	สีขาว
yellow	sěe lěuarng	สีเหลือง

Bargaining and payment

How much?	tâo rài
… per dozen	lǒh lá …
… per kilo	loh lá …
… per pack	hòr lá …
… per metre	máyt lá …
… per yard (for silk)	lǎr lá …
It's too expensive	pairng Pai
Could you lower the price?	lót dâi mái
How about … baht?	… bàrt dâi mái
Do you take …?	jài Pehn … dâi mái
… credit cards	… bàt kray-dìt …
… traveller's cheques	… chéhk dern tarng …
… (US) dollars	… (yoo-áyt) don-lâr …
Sorry, I don't have any change	mâi mee ngern yôy
A receipt, please	kǒr bai-sèht dûay
My change, please	kǒr ngern torn dûay

General phrases

ráp a-rai kráp/ká	Can I help you?
mee kráp/kâ	Yes, we have some
mâi mee kráp/kâ	No, we don't have any
mòt láirw	We've sold out/We're out of stock
lorng rárn èurn	You may try another shop
ráp a-rai èek mái	Anything else?
rárn Pìt láirw	We are closed now

Buying

kŏrng pôo-chai rĕur pôo-yĭng	For a man or a woman?
bàirp nǎi dee kráp/ká	Which style would you like?
sěe nǎi dee kráp/ká	Which colour would you like?
ber/sái nǎi dee kráp/ká	Which size would you like?
jà lorng mái kráp/ká	Would you like to try it on?
chôrp mái kráp/ká	Do you like it/them?
hòr kŏrng kwǎn mái kráp/ká	Would you like it/them gift-wrapped?

Bargaining and payment

mâi bàirng kǎi	We don't sell them separately
lót mâi dâi	Sorry, no reductions
mâi pairng ròrk	It's not expensive
bàt kray-dìt kŏr kít pêrm	We have to add on a surcharge if you pay by credit card
mee bai yôy mái	Do you have any smaller change?

Business Trips

▌ You'll probably be doing business with the help of interpreters or in a language everyone speaks, but you may need a few Thai phrases to cope at a company's reception desk.

▌ Business hours in Thailand are normally from 9 a.m. to 5 p.m. with a one-hour lunch break at 12 noon. Some companies in Bangkok operate a flexi-time system for their staff, so that they can avoid the city's notorious traffic jams. In this case, working hours may be anything between 7 a.m. and 7 p.m., with staff coming and going at different times. If you are meeting people, check their working hours.

▌ Working days in the private sector are from Monday to Friday and sometimes include Saturday morning as well.

▌ Public sector hours are from 8.30 a.m. to 4.30 p.m. Monday to Friday, with the same lunch hour as the private sector.

Useful signs

ทางเข้า	tarng kão	entrance
ทางออก	tarng òrk	exit
ทางออกฉุกเฉิน	tarng òrk chùk chěrn	emergency exit
ทางหนีไฟ	tarng něe fai	fire exit
ผลัก	plàk	push
ดึง	deuhng	pull
ติดต่อสอบถาม	Tìt-Tòr sòrp-tǎrm	reception
ประชาสัมพันธ์	Pra-char sǎm-pan	information
เวลาทำการ	way-lar tam-garn	office hours
เฉพาะพนักงาน	cha-pó pa-nák-ngarn	staff only
ห้ามเข้า	hârm kão	no entry

ห้ามสูบบุหรี่	hârm sòop bu-rèe	no smoking
ห้ามขายของ	hârm kǎi kǒrng	no salesmen
ชั้น	chán	floor
บันได	ban-dai	stairs
ลิฟต์	líf	lift
(ลิฟต์) เสีย	(líf) sǐa	(lift) out of order
รปภ.	ror-Por-por	security

Useful words

business card/name card	narm-bàt
company	bor-ri-sàt
company director	gam-ma-garn bor-ri-sàt
director	pôo-am-nuay-garn
managing director	gam-ma-garn pôo-jàt-garn
manager	pôo-jàt-garn
secretary	lay-kǎr (-nú-garn)

You may want to say

Good morning/Good afternoon/ Good evening	sa-wàt-dee kráp/kâ
I'd like to see ..., please	kǒr póp ... kráp/kâ
... Mr Pisit ...	... kun pí-sìt ...
... Mrs Yindee ...	... kun yin-dee ...
... Miss Saijai ...	... kun sǎi-jai ...
... the export manager ...	... pôo-jàt-garn fài sòng òrk ...
My name is ...	pǒm/di-chán chêur ...
I work for ...	pǒm/di-chán mar jàrk ...
Here's my card	nêe narm-bàt kǒrng pǒm/di-chán

I have an appointment with …	pŏm/di-chán mee nát gàp …
I haven't got an appointment	pŏm/di-chán mâi dâi nát wái
I'd like to make an appointment with …	pŏm/di-chán kŏr nát gàp …
What is his/her name?	káo chêur a-rai kráp/ká
When will he/she be back?	káo jà glàp mar mêuar rài kráp/ká
Can I leave a message?	sàng kôr kwarm wái dâi mái
Can you ask him/her to call me?	chûay bòrk káo hâi toh tĕuhng pŏm/dichán dâi mái
I'm staying at the Imperial Hotel	pŏm/di-chán pák yòo têe rohng-rairm im-pee-rîan
Room 1078	hôrng ber nèuhng-sŏon-jèht-Pàirt
The telephone number is …	toh-ra-sàp ber …
Where is his/her office?	hôrng tam-ngarn kŏrng káo yòo têe năi
I'm here for …	pŏm/di-chán mar rûam …
… the conference	… garn Pra-chum
… the exhibition	… ngarn ní-tát-sa-garn
… the trade fair	… ngarn sa-dairng sĭn-kár
I need …	pŏm/di-chán Tôrng-garn …
… someone to type a letter for me	… kon chûay pim jòt-măi
… a photocopy of this	… tài àyk-ga-sărn bai née
… an interpreter	… lârm
I need to make a phone call	pŏm/di-chán Tôrng-garn toh-ra-sàp
I need to send this …	pŏm/di-chán Tôrng-garn sòng an née …
… by courier	… Pai tarng koo-ria
… by fax	… Pai tarng fàihk
… by post	… Pai tarng Prai-sa-nee

Reception

kun chêur a-rai kráp/ká	Your name, please?
mar jàrk nǎi kráp/ká	The name of your company, please?
nát wái rěur Plào kráp/ká	Do you have an appointment?
ror dǐaw ná kráp/ká	One moment, please
kun pí-sìt mâi yòo kráp/kâ	Mr Pisit isn't in
kun yin-dee jà glàp mar …	Mrs Yindee will be back …
… Torn sìp mohng	… at 10 o'clock
… Torn bài sǎrm mohng	… at 3 p.m.
… èek krêuhng chûa-mohng	… in half an hour
… èek nèuhng chûa-mohng	… in an hour
káo gam-lang ror yòo kráp/kâ	He/She's expecting you
káo gam-lang mar kráp/kâ	He/She's just coming
chern nâng gòrn kráp/kâ	Please sit down

Directions

chern kâo Pai dâi kráp/kâ	Go in, please
chern tarng née kráp/kâ	This way, please
kêuhn líf Pai chán …	Take the lift to the …th floor
yòo chán sèe	It's on the fourth floor
yòo chán hâr	It's on the fifth floor
Pra-Too râirk	It's the first door
Pra-Too têe sǒrng	It's the second door
tarng sái	On the left
tarng kwǎr	On the right
hôrng ber …	It's room number …
chern kráp/kâ	Come in!

Sightseeing

▌ Foreigners pay a little more than the locals to get into government-run national museums, palaces and historical parks. The opening hours of these places are generally the same as government office hours. They open at weekends and are closed on two other days of the week instead. Check locally, to be on the safe side.

▌ The Grand Palace in Bangkok and all temples in Thailand require appropriate dress. You will be refused entry if the guards consider your style of dress unsuitable.

▌ Sightseeing tours by coach with English-speaking guides are available in many cities and tourist areas.

▌ You can also hire a local English-speaking guide to show you around. Remember to negotiate the fee first.

Useful signs

เปิด	Pèrt	open
ปิด	Pìt	closed
ห้ามเข้า	hârm kâo	no entry
ห้ามสูบบุหรี่	hârm sòop bu-rèe	no smoking
ห้ามถ่ายรูป	hârm tài rôop	no photographs
ห้ามใช้แฟลช	hârm chái flàiht	no flash photography
กรุณาอย่าแตะ	ga-ru-nar yàr Tàih	please do not touch
กรุณาถอดรองเท้า	ga-ru-nar tòrt rorng-táo	please take off your shoes

Opening times

When is the museum open?	pí-pít-ta-pan Pèrt gèe mohng
What time does the … close?	… Pìt gèe mohng
… temple …	wát …
… (historical) park …	ùt-ta-yarn (Pra-wàt-Ti-sàrt) …
Is it open on Sundays?	Pèrt wan ar-tít rěur Plào
What days (of the week) does it close?	Pìt wan a-rai bârng
Is it open to the public?	Pèrt hâi kon tûa Pai kâo chom mái
Can I visit the …?	Pai chom … dâi mái

Visiting places

One ticket, please	nèuhng kon kráp/kâ
Two tickets, please	sŏrng kon kráp/kâ
Two adults	pôo-yài sŏrng kon
(And) one child	(gàp) dèhk nèuhng kon
Are there any reductions for …?	… lót rar-kar mái
… children	dèhk …
… groups	mar Pehn ka-ná …
… students	nák sèuhk-săr
Can I take photos?	tài rôop dâi mái
Can I use a flash?	chái flàiht dâi mái
Could you take a photo of me, please?	chûay tài rôop pŏm/di-chán dâi mái kráp/ká

Excursions

Are there any excursions to …?	mee jàt tua Pai … mái
What time does it leave?	tua òrk gèe mohng
How long does the tour last?	chái way-lar narn táo-rài

What time does it get back?	ja glàp tĕuhng gèe mohng
Where does it leave from?	tua òrk jàrk têe nǎi
Can you pick us up from our hotel?	Pai ráp têe rohng-rairm dâi mái
Does the guide speak English?	gái pôot ang-grìt rĕur Plào
How much is it?	kâr tua tâo rài
Is it all-inclusive?	ruam mòt châi mái
Is the meal included in the price?	ruam ar-hǎrn dûay mái

You may hear

Pèrt túk wan	We open every day
yók wáyn wan jan	Except Mondays
rót òrk sìp mohng jàrk …	The tour leaves at ten o'clock from …
fa-ràng … bàrt	… baht for foreigners
kon tai … bàrt	… baht for Thais
Tàirng-Tua yàrng née hârm kâo	You cannot come in dressed like that
tòrt rorng-táo wái Trong nán	Please leave your shoes over there

Health

█ If you need medical attention, an appointment to see a doctor at a private hospital or clinic can easily be made. The cost of medical attention at these private institutions can be expensive, so medical insurance is essential. Treatment at public hospitals is free (you pay only the cost of medicines), but they are very crowded and are best avoided unless in an emergency.

█ Most doctors can communicate adequately in English. For minor problems, you can seek advice and purchase medicines, including antibiotics and penicillin, without a prescription from a chemist's, which by law has to be supervised by a qualified pharmacist.

Useful signs

รถพยาบาล	rót pa-yar-barn	ambulance
โรงพยาบาล	rohng-pa-yar-barn	hospital
คลีนิค	klee-nìk	clinic
แผนกผู้ป่วยนอก	pa-nàirk pôo-Pùay nôrk	out-patients department
อุบัติเหตุ	pa-nàirk ù-bàt-Tì-hàyt	accidents
ฉุกเฉิน	chùk-chěrn	emergency
ตรวจสายตา	Trùat sǎi-Tar	eye tests
ร้านขายยา	rárn kǎi yar	chemist

Parts of the body

ankle	kôr táo	ข้อเท้า
appendix	sâi Tîng	ไส้ติ่ง
arm	kǎirn	แขน

back	lăng	หลัง
bladder	gra-pó Pàt-sa-wá	กระเพาะปัสสาวะ
blood	lêuart	เลือด
body	rârng gai	ร่างกาย
bone	gra-dòok	กระดูก
bottom	gôn	ก้น
bowels	gra-pó lam-sâi	กระเพาะลำไส้
breast	Tâo-nom	เต้านม
cartilage	gra-dòok òrn	กระดูกอ่อน
chest	nâr-òk	หน้าอก
chin	karng	คาง
ear	hŏo	หู
elbow	kôr sòrk	ข้อศอก
eye	Tar	ตา
face	bai-nâr	ใบหน้า
finger	níw meur	นิ้วมือ
foot	táo	เท้า
genitals	a-wai-ya-wá sèurp-pan	อวัยวะสืบพันธุ์
gland	Tòm	ต่อม
hair	pŏm	ผม
hand	meur	มือ
head	hŭa	หัว
heart	hŭa-jai	หัวใจ
heel	sôn táo	ส้นเท้า
hip	sa-pôhk	สะโพก
jaw	kăr-gan-grai	ขากรรไกร
joint	gra-dòok kôr-Tòr	กระดูกข้อต่อ
kidney	Tai	ไต
knee	hŭa-kào	หัวเข่า
leg	kăr	ขา
ligament	ehn	เอ็น

115

lip	rim-fěe-Pàrk	ริมฝีปาก
liver	Tàp	ตับ
lung	Pòrt	ปอด
mouth	Pàrk	ปาก
muscle	glârm-néuar	กล้ามเนื้อ
nail	léhp	เล็บ
neck	kor	คอ
nerve	Pra-sàrt	ประสาท
nose	ja-mòok	จมูก
penis	ong-ka-chárt	องคชาติ
rectum	chông ta-warn	ช่องทวาร
rib	sêe-krohng	ซี่โครง
shin	nâr-kâirng	หน้าแข้ง
shoulder	hǔa-lài	หัวไหล่
skin	pǐw-nǎng	ผิวหนัง
spine	gra-dòok sǎn-lǎng	กระดูกสันหลัง
stomach	tórng	ท้อง
tendon	ehn	เอ็น
testicles	an-tá	อัณฑะ
thigh	Tôn kǎr	ต้นขา
throat	lam-kor	ลำคอ
thumb	níw hǔa mâir-meur	นิ้วหัวแม่มือ
toe	níw táo	นิ้วเท้า
tongue	lín	ลิ้น
tonsils	ton-sin	ทอนซิล
tooth	fan	ฟัน
vagina	chông klôrt	ช่องคลอด
waist	ehw	เอว
wrist	kôr meur	ข้อมือ

Diseases and medical problems

AIDS	àyt	เอคส์
anaemia	loh-hìt jarng	โลหิตจาง
appendicitis	sâi-Tǐng àk-sàyp	ไส้ติ่งอักเสบ
asthma	rôhk hèurt	โรคหืด
cancer	ma-rehng	มะเร็ง
chickenpox	ee-sùk-ee-săi	อีสุกอีใส
cholera	a-hì-war	อหิวาต์
diabetes	bao-wǎrn	เบาหวาน
dysentery	rôhk bìt	โรคบิด
epilepsy	lom-bâr-mǒo	ลมบ้าหมู
flu	kâi wàt	ไข้หวัด
food poisoning	ar-hǎrn Pehn pít	อาหารเป็นพิษ
German measles	hàt yer-ra-man	หัดเยอรมัน
hepatitis	Tàp àk-sàyp	ตับอักเสบ
indigestion	ar-hǎrn mâi yôy	อาหารไม่ย่อย
jaundice	dee-sârn	ดีซ่าน
malaria	mar-lar-ria	มาลาเรีย
measles	rôhk hàt	โรคหัด
migraine	mai-grayn	ไมเกรน
mumps	karng toom	คางทูม
plague	gar-la-rôhk	กาฬโรค
pneumonia	Pòrt buam	ปอดบวม
prickly heat	pòt	ผด
rabies	rôhk glua nárm	โรคกลัวน้ำ
rheumatism	rôhk kǎi-kôr	โรคไขข้อ
smallpox	kâi tor-ra-pít	ไข้ทรพิษ
stomach ulcer	plǎir nai gra-pró	แผลในกระเพาะ
tetanus	bàrt-ta-yák	บาดทะยัก
tuberculosis	wan-na-rôhk	วัณโรค
yellow fever	kâi lěuarng	ไข้เหลือง

General phrases

There's been an accident	gèrt ù-bàt-Tì-hàyt
I need a doctor	pŏm/di-chán Tôrng-garn mŏr
Please call a doctor	chûay Tarm mŏr dûay
How soon can the doctor be here?	mŏr mar dâi mêuar rài
I'm pregnant	di-chán mee tórng

Seeing the doctor

I have a heart condition	pŏm/di-chán Pehn rôhk hŭa-jai
I had a heart attack in 1990	pŏm/di-chán koei hŭa-jai wai nai Pee nèuhng-gâo-gâo-sŏon
I have high blood pressure	pŏm/di-chán kwarm dan sŏong
I have high blood pressure	pŏm/di-chán kwarm dan tàm
I'm a diabetic	pŏm/di-chán Pehn bao-wărn
I'm allergic to ...	pŏm/di-chán páir ...
My blood group is ...	pŏm/di-chán glùm lêuart ...

Symptoms

I feel unwell	pŏm/di-chán mâi sa-bai
It hurts here	jèhp Trong née
My ... hurts/hurt	Pùat or jèhp ...
I've got a ...	Pùat ...
... headache	... hŭa
... stomach ache	... tórng
There's ... here	Trong née ...
... a lump ...	... Pehn gôrn
... a rash ...	... Pehn pèurn
... a swelling ...	... buam

118

I've got a wound here	Trong née Pehn plǎir
I've got a sore throat	jèhp kor
I've got a temperature	pehn kâi
I feel dizzy	wian hǔa
I've been sick	ar-jian
I've got diarrhoea	tórng sǐa
I've got constipation	tórng pòok
I can't sleep	norn mâi làp
I can't breathe	hǎi jai mâi sa-dùak
I have a cough	ai
My ... is bleeding	... lêuart òrk
I've broken my ...	... hàk
I've sprained my ...	... kléht
I've cut myself	tòok kǒrng mee kom bàrt
I've burnt myself	tòok fai lûak
I've scalded myself	tòok nárm rórn lûak
I've been stung by an insect	tòok ma-lairng Tòy
I've been bitten by a dog	tòok mǎr gàt
I've been scratched by a cat	tòok mairw kùan

At the dentist's

I need to see a dentist	Tôrng garn mǒr fan
I've got toothache	Pùat fan
This tooth hurts	Pùat fan sêe née
I've broken a tooth	fan hàk
I've lost a filling	têe ùt fan lùt
I've lost a crown/cap	têe krôrp fan hǎi
Can you fix it (temporarily)?	chûay tam fan (bàirp chûa-krao) dâi mái
Can you give me an injection?	chûay chèet yar char dâi mái?
I've broken my dentures	fan Plorm an née hàk
Can you repair them?	chûay sôrm dâi mái

At the chemist's (asking for basic medicines)

I want to buy some …	kŏr séur …
… antibiotics	… yar gâir nŏrng or yar Pa-Tì-chee-wa-ná
… antihistamine	… yar tar gâir pèurn kan
… antiseptic	… yar kâr chéuar
… aspirins	… áirt-pai-rin
… cold relief	… yar gâir wàt
… constipation relief	… yar gâir tórng pòok
… cough medicine	… yar gâir ai
… decongestant nasal spray	… yar pôn ja-mòok
… diarrhoea tablets	… yar gâir tórng sĭa
… indigestion relief	… yar gâir tórng èurt
… insect repellant	… yar gan ma-lairng
… painkillers	… yar gâir Pùat
… sleeping pills	… yar norn làp
… (sticking) plasters	… plárt-sa-Têr Pìt plăir
… throat lozenges	… yar om gâir jèhp kor
… tranquillizers	… yar ra-ngáp Pra-sàrt
I want it in … form	kŏr bàirp …
… capsule …	… káihp-soon
… cream/ointment …	… yar tar
… liquid/syrup …	… yar nárm
… tablet …	… yar méht
How do I apply it?/How often do I apply it?	chái yar yàrng rai
How do I take it?	gin yar yàrng rai
How many do I take?	gin yar gèe méht
Before or after meals?	gòrn rĕur lăng ar-hărn

At the doctor's – General phrases

jèhp têe năi	Where does it hurt?
Trong née jèhp mái	Does it hurt here?
jèhp mârk mái	Does it hurt a lot?
Pehn yàrng née narn tâo rai láirw	How long have you been feeling like this?
ar-yú tâo rài	How old are you?
wan née gin a-rai mar	What have you eaten today?
chûay âr Pàrk dûay	Open your mouth, please
tòrt sêuar dûay	Take your top off, please
tòrt garng-gayng/gra-Prohng dûay	Take your trousers/skirt off, please
Tôrng Trùat pai nai	I need to examine you internally
norn bon Tiang dûay	Lie down over there, please
Tàirng-Tua dái	You can get dressed again

At the doctor's – treatment

gin yar a-rai yòo rĕur Plào	Are you taking any medicines?
páir yar a-rai rĕur Plào	Are you allergic to any medicine?
chái in-soo-lin ka-nàrt năi yòo	What dose of insulin are you taking?
chèet yar gan bàrt-ta-yák mar rĕur Plào	Have you been vaccinated against tetanus?
mee ar-garn Tìt chéuar	There's an infection
Tôrng chèet yar	I'm going to give you an injection
Tôrng éhk-sa-ray	I'm going to send you for an X-ray
Tôrng Trùat Tua-yàrng lêurt/Pàt-sa-wá	I need a blood/urine sample
ar-hărn Pehn pít	You have food poisoning
hŭa-jai wai	You've had a heart attack
Tôrng pák pòrn	You must rest

121

Tôrng norn pák … wan	You must stay in bed for … days
èek … wan glàp mar hăr mŏr mài	You must come back in … days' time
Tôrng norn rohng-pa-yar-barn	You will have to go to hospital
mee ar-garn hàk/klêuarn/kléht	It's broken/dislocated/sprained
Tôrng kăo fèuark	I'm going to put it in plaster
mâi Pehn a-rai mârk	It's nothing serious
mâi Pehn a-rai loei	There's nothing wrong with you
ja kĭan bai sàng yar hâi	I'm going to give you a prescription

At the dentist's

chûay âr Pàrk dûay	Open your mouth, please
Tôrng ùt fan	You need a filling
Tôrng tŏrn fan sêe née òrk	I'll have to take this tooth out
ja chèet yar char hâi	I'll give you an injection

At the chemist's

mee ar-garn yàrng rai	What are the symptoms?

Dosages

nèuhng méht	One tablet/capsule
sŏrng méht	Two tablets/capsules
nèuhng chórn Tó	One tablespoon
sŏrng chórn char	Two teaspoons
tar yar hâi tûa	Rub it (i.e. the cream/ointment) all over
wan lá sŏrng/sărm kráng	Twice/three times a day
gòrn ar-harn	Before meals
lăng ar-harn	After meals
gòrn norn	Before going to bed at night

Laundry

▌Because of the high humidity and hot weather in Thailand, there are many shops offering a laundry service for next to nothing. You will find them mainly in the areas of Bangkok and the other main cities where there are many tourist hotels and guest houses. The service is efficient. Normally, if you send your laundry in before mid-morning, your clothes will be ready for collection – washed and neatly ironed – by late afternoon on the same day. You may of course use your hotel's laundry service if they offer one, but expect to pay over the odds.

Useful signs

รับซักรีด	ráp sák rêet	Laundry service
รับซักแห้ง	ráp sák hâirng	Dry-cleaning service
ส่งเช้าได้เย็น	sòng cháo dâi yehn	Same day service

You may want to say

I'd like to have this/these … washed	Tôrng-garn sák …
I'd like to have this/these … dry-cleaned	Tôrng-garn sák hâirng …
… blouse …	… sêuar
… dress …	… sêuar chút
… jacket …	… sêuar jáihk-gêht
… knickers/underpants …	… garng-gayng nai
… shirt …	… sêuar chért
… skirt …	… gra-Prohng
… socks …	… tŭng táo

123

… suit …	… sòot
… T-shirt …	… sêuar tee-chért *or* sêuar yêurt
… trousers …	… garng-gayng
… underwear …	… chút chán nai
… vest …	… sêuar glârm
This one is made of …	an née tam dûay …
… cotton	… pâr fâi
… silk	… pâr măi
This one is for …	an née …
… cold washing	… sák nárm yehn
… hand washing	… sák meur
… warm washing	… sák nárm ùn
This one shouldn't be ironed	an née mâi Tôrng rêet
When can I collect them?	jà dâi mêuar-rài
Can you do it at once?	tam hâi dùan dâi mái
Do you have an express service?	mee bor-ri-garn dùan mái
What is the charge?	kít ra-kar yàrng-rai

Tua lá … bàrt	… baht per item
kôo lá … bàrt	… baht per pair
sòng chár Pai	It's too late now
prûng née dâi	You can collect it/them tomorrow
… Torn cháo	… morning
… Torn tîang	… noon
… Torn bài	… afternoon
… Torn yehn	… evening
táng-mòt … bàrt	That's … baht altogether

124

Emergencies, problems and complaints

▌ Accidents and crimes should be reported to the police, who wear khaki uniforms. In tourist areas, there is a special Tourist Police Unit, recognizable by the TP badge on the uniform. Police officers in this unit speak English.

▌ Although it is normal practice to report any crime or traffic accident at the nearest police station, you may find a police booth nearby, where you can make the initial report. The police officer at the booth may be able to help you on the spot or will make the necessary arrangements for you to go to the police station.

The emergency telephone number for Bangkok and surrounding provinces sharing Bangkok's telephone area code is 191.

▌ There is *no* nationwide emergency telephone number in Thailand. Unless you are in the area covered by Bangkok's telephone area code, you have to dial **13** and ask the telephone operator for the numbers of the emergency service in the area. **13** is the number of the telephone directory enquiry service.

▌ Other useful nationwide telephone numbers are:

100 – International telephone operator service

101 – National long-distance telephone operator service (including calls to Malaysia and Lao)

193 – Highways Police

Useful signs

สถานีตำรวจ   sa-tăr-nee Tam-rùat   police station

You may want to say

General phrases

Help!	chûay dûay
Fire!	fai mâi
Police!	Tam-rùat
Thief!	ka-mohy
Look out!	rá-wang
The lift is stuck	líf kárng
Where is the (nearest) …?	… (glâi têe sùt) yòo têe năi
… police station	sa-tăr-nee Tam-rùat …
… police booth	Pôm yarm …
… hospital	rohng-pa-yar-barn
Can you help me?	chûay pŏm/di-chán dûay kráp/kâ
Can I speak to the manager?	kŏr póp pôo-jàt-garn
Can you fix it (immediately)?	chûay sôrm (tan-tee) dâi mái
When can you fix it?	sôrm dâi mêuar rài
The … doesn't work	… mâi tam ngarn
I need …	kŏr …

At hotels, guest houses etc.

There isn't any …	mâi mee …
… (hot) water	… nárm (rórn)
… electricity	… fai fár
… soap	… sa-bòo

... toilet paper	... gra-dàrt cham-rá
There isn't a towel	mâi mee pâr-chét-Tua
There's no plug in the ...	... mâi mee Plák
... bath	àrng àrp-nárm ...
... wash basin	àrng lárng nâr ...
I need another ...	kŏr ... èek
... blanket	... pâr hòm
... pillowcase	... Plòrk mŏrn
The shower doesn't work	fàk-bua mâi tam ngarn
The toilet doesn't flush	chák-krôhk mâi long
The light bulb's gone	lòrt fai kàrt
The bed is broken	Tiang pang
The lock's broken	lók sĭa
I can't open/close ...	Pèrt/Pìt ... mâi dâi
... the door	... Pra-Too ...
... the window	... nâr-Tàrng ...
There's a lot of noise	mee sĭang róp-guan mârk
Can I change my room?	kŏr Plìan hôrng dâi mái

Bars and restaurants

Where's my order?	Tóh née yang mâi dâi ar-hărn
This isn't cooked	an née tam mâi sùk
This is burnt	an née mâi
This is cold	an née yehn chêurt
This smells bad	glìn mâi dee
This tastes strange	rót Plàirk-Plàirk
The glass is cracked	gâirw mee roy ráo
The spoon's dirty	chórn sòk-ga-Pròk
I didn't order this	an née mâi dâi sàng
I ordered ...	pŏm/di-chán sàng ...
There's a mistake on the bill	sŏng-săi wâr kít ngern pìt

Shops

I bought this (yesterday)	an née séur (mêuar warn née)
I want to return this	kŏr keurn an née
I want to exchange this	kŏr Plìan an née
There's a hole	mee roo
There's a stain/mark	mee roy-Pêuarn
It's torn	mee roy-kàrt
Can I have a refund?	kŏr ngern keurn dâi mái
Here's the receipt	nêe bai-sèht
My change, please	kŏr ngern-torn dûay
I think you've made a mistake	ngern-torn mâi króp

Losing things

I have lost …	pŏm/di-chán tam … hăi
… my bag	… gra-Păo …
… my driving licence	… bai kàp-kèe
… my wallet	… gra-Păo ngern …
I have forgotten …	pŏm/di-chán leurm …
… my key	… gun-jair
… my ticket	… Tŭa

Crimes

I want to report … (to police)	kŏr jâirng kwarm …
… a crime	… hàyt rái
… a theft	… kŏng tòok ka-mohy
… some lost property	… kŏng hăi
I've been robbed	tòok Plôn
Someone's stolen my money	tòok ka-mohy ngern
I have been raped	tòok kòm-kĕurn

Accidents

I want to report an accident	kŏr jâirng ù-bàt-Ti-hàyt
There's been a car crash	mee hàyt rót chon
He/she crashed/bumped into me	káo chon pŏm/di-chán
He/she cut across me	káo Tàt nâr pŏm/di-chán
I was in my lane	pŏm/di-chán yòo nai layn
I was stationary	pŏm/di-chán jòrt yòo chŏei-chŏei
I was crossing the road (at the zebra-crossing)	pŏm/di-chán gam-lang kârm ta-nŏn (Trong tarng már-lai)
He/she didn't stop	káo mâi yùt
He/she didn't give a signal	káo mâi hâi săn-yarn
He/she jumped the red light	káo fàr fai dairng
I fell over	pŏm/di-chán hòk-lóm
I fell downstairs	pŏm/di-chán Tòk ban-dai
I fell off ...	pŏm/di-chán Tòk ...
... my bicycle	... jàk-gra-yarn
... the bus	... rót-may

You may hear

Helpful and unhelpful phrases

ror dĭaw kráp/kâ	Just a moment, please
jà tam yarng dee têe sùt	I'll do everything I can
dĭaw ao mar hâi kráp/kâ	I'll bring it right away
jà sôrm hâi tan-tee	I'll fix it immediately
jà tam hâi mài	We'll prepare a new dish for you
tam mâi dâi	It's not possible
chûay a-rai mâi dâi	There's nothing I can do
rao mâi ráp-pit-chôrp	We're not responsible for this
kun kuan Pai jâirng Tam-rùat	You should report it to the police

Questions you may be asked

Shops

séur mar mêuar rài	When did you buy it?
mee bai-sèht mái	Do you have a receipt?

Police – crime & accidents

hàyt gèrt têe năi	Where did it happen?
hàyt gèrt mêuar rài	When did it happen?
rêuarng Pehn yarng rai	What happened?
tam hăi mêuar rài	When did you lose it?
gra-Păo bàirp năi	What does your bag/purse/wallet look like?
tam dûay a-rai	What's it made of?
a-rai hăi Pai bârng	What have you lost?
mee kon rái gèe kon	How many robbers/muggers were there?
hĕhn Tua kon rái mái	Did you see who did it?
jam nâr dâi mái	Could you identify them?
mee krai Pehn a-rai mái	Is anyone hurt?

Police – about yourself

chêur a-rai	What is your name?
săn-chârt a-rai	What is your nationality?
pák têe năi	Where are you staying?
hôrng ber a-rai	What is your room number?
párt-sa-Pòrt ber a-rai	What is your passport number?
mee Pra-gan mái	Are you insured?
sehn chêur Trong née	Please sign here

Conversion tables

Linear measurements

centimetre(s)	sehn-Ti-máyt or sehn : cm
metre(s)	máyt : m
kilometre(s)	gi-loh máyt or gi-loh : km
10 cm = 4 inches	1 inch = 2.54 cm
50 cm = 19.6 inches	1 foot = 30 cm
1 metre = 39.37 inches	1 yard = 0.91 m
100 metres = 110 yards	
1 km = 0.62 miles	1 mile = 1.61 km

To convert km to miles: divide by 8 and multiply by 5

miles to km: divide by 5 and multiply by 8

Miles		Kilometres
0.6	1	1.6
1.2	2	3.2
1.9	3	4.8
2.5	4	6.4
3	5	8
6	10	16
12	20	32
19	30	48
25	40	64
31	50	80
62	100	161
68	110	177
93	150	241

Liquid measures

litre   lít

1 litre = 1.8 pints   1 pint = 0.57 litres

5 litres = 1.1 gallons   1 gallon = 4.55 litres

Gallons		Litres
0.2	1	4.5
0.4	2	9
0.7	3	13.6
0.9	4	18
1.1	5	23
2.2	10	45.5

Weights

gram   gram : g

100 grams   nèuhng kèet

200 grams   sŏrng kèet

500 grams   hâr kèet or krêurng gi-loh

kilo   gi-loh or gi-loh gram : kg

100 g = 3.5 oz   1 oz = 28 g

200 g = 7 oz $1/4$ lb = 113 g

$1/2$ kilo = 1.1 lb $1/2$ lb = 225 g

1 kilo = 2.2 lb   1 lb = 450 g

Pounds		Kilograms
2.2	1	0.45 (450)
4.4	2	0.9 (900)
6.6	3	1.4 (1400)

8.8	4	1.8 (1800)
11	5	2.3 (2300)
22	10	4.5 (4500)

Area

In Thailand, land is measured in **'râi'** - ไร่. There are 2.5 **râi** to an acre or 6.25 **râi** to a hectare. One **râi** consists of 400 square **'war'** - โว่าl or 400 **'Ta-rarng war'**- โตารางวาl as it is expressed in Thailand.

To convert

acres to **râi**: divide by 2 and multiply by 5

râi to acres: divide by 5 and multiply by 2

Acres		**Râi**
0.4	1	2.5
2	5	12.5
4	10	25
20	50	125
40	100	250

Shoe sizes

UK	3	4	5	6	7	8	9	10	11
Thailand	36	37	38	39	41	42	43	44	45

▌ Some public holidays in Thailand have fixed dates and others vary, depending on whether they follow the solar or lunar calendar. Since all Buddhist religious holidays follow the lunar calendar, they vary from year to year. In certain provinces in the south of Thailand where there are sizeable Muslim communities, certain Islamic holidays are also observed.

▌ Unless you want to contact a business or government office, you may not even notice if it is a public holiday because life goes on as normal, including in shopping and entertainment places. Police stations and emergency hospital wards stay open all year round, holiday or not.

▌ The dates of the Buddhist religious holidays shown here are for a guideline only. You should check with the locals whether there are any public holidays during the duration of your stay in Thailand.

1 January	– New Year's Day
Mid to late February	– Maka Pucha Day (Buddhist religious day)
6 April	– Chakri Dynasty Day
12-14 April	– Songkran Days (Traditional Thai New Year holidays)
1 May	– National Labour Day
5 May	– King Bhumipol's Coronation Day
Mid to late May	– Visaka Pucha Day (Buddhist religious day)
1 July	– Mid Year Holiday (for banks only)
Mid to late July	– Khao Pansa Day (Buddhist Lent) (Buddhist religious day)
12 August	– Queen Sirikit's Birthday
23 October	– King Chulalongkorn Commemoration Day
5 December	– King Bhumipol's Birthday
10 December	– Constitution Day
25 December	– Christmas Day (private sectors only)
31 December	– End of Year Day

Useful addresses

In the UK

Royal Thai Embassy

30 Queen's Gate
London SW7 5JB
Tel: 071-589 0173
Visa section: 071-589 2857

Tourist Authority of Thailand (TAT)

49 Albemarle Street
London W1X 3FE
Tel: 0171-499 7679
Tel: 353 1 78 15 99

In Thailand

The British Embassy
1031 Witthayu (Wireless) Road
Bangkok 10500
Tel: 66-2-253 0191

สถานทูตอังกฤษ
๑๐๓๑ ถนนวิทยุ
กรุงเทพฯ ๑๐๕๐๐
โทร. ๖๖-๒-๒๕๓ ๐๑๙๑

The US Embassy
95 Witthayu (Wireless) Road
Bangkok 10500
Tel: 66-2-252 5040

สถานทูตอเมริกัน
๙๕ ถนนวิทยุ
กรุงเทพฯ ๑๐๕๐๐
โทร. ๖๖-๒-๒๕๒ ๕๐๔๐

A

a, an (no articles in Thai)		
about	Pra-marn	ประมาณ
above	kârng bon	ข้างบน
to accept *(admit)*	yorm-ráp	ยอมรับ
(receive)	ráp	รับ
accident	ù-bàt-Tì-hàyt	อุบัติเหตุ
account *(bank)*	ban-chee	บัญชี
ache	Pùat	ปวด
across *(go over)*	kârm	ข้าม
(be in the way)	kwǎrng	ขวาง
adaptor	krêuarng Plairng fai-fár	เครื่องแปลงไฟฟ้า
address	têe-yòo	ที่อยู่
adhesive tape	táyp gao	เทปกาว
admission charge	kâr kâo chom	ค่าเข้าชม
adult	pôo-yài	ผู้ใหญ่
to advertise, advertisement	kôht-sa-nar	โฆษณา
aeroplane	krêuarng bin	เครื่องบิน
afraid	glua	กลัว
after	lǎng	หลัง
afternoon	Torn bài	ตอนบ่าย
aftershave	nám-yar lǎng gohn nùat	น้ำยาหลังโกนหนวด
afterwards	tee lǎng	ทีหลัง
again	èek	อีก
against	Tòr-Târn	ต่อต้าน
age	ar-yú	อายุ

ago	gòrn	ก่อน
to agree	Tòk-long	ตกลง
air	ar-gàrt	อากาศ
air-conditioning	krêuarng air	เครื่องแอร์
airline	săi-garn-bin	สายการบิน
airport	sa-nărm-bin	สนามบิน
alarm clock	nar-lí-gar Plùk	นาฬิกาปลุก
alcohol	lâo	เหล้า
alive	mee chee-wít	มีชีวิต
all	táng-mòt	ทั้งหมด
to allow	yorm	ยอม
almost	gèuarp	เกือบ
alone	kon diaw	คนเดียว
already	láirw	แล้ว
also	dûay	ด้วย
although	máir-wâr	แม้ว่า
ambulance	rót pa-yar-barn	รถพยาบาล
anaesthetic	yar sa-lòp	ยาสลบ
and	láih	และ
angry	gròht	โกรธ
animal	sàt	สัตว์
annoyed	ram-karn	รำคาญ
another	an èurn	อันอื่น
to answer	Tòrp	ตอบ
answer	kam-Tòrp	คำตอบ
antique (n)	kŏrng gào	ของเก่า
apartment	a-párt-máyn	อพาร์ตเม้นท์
appointment	nát	นัด
approximately	Pra-marn	ประมาณ
to argue	tĭang	เถียง
around	rôrp	รอบ

to arrest	jàp	จับ
to arrive	mar těuhng	มาถึง
art	sǐn-la-Pà	ศิลป
artist	sǐn-la-Pin	ศิลปิน
ashtray	têe kìa bu-rèe	ที่เขี่ยบุหรี่
to ask	tǎrm	ถาม
at	têe	ที่
to attack	tam-rái	ทำร้าย
attractive	sǔay	สวย
aunt (*elder sister of mother/father*)	Pâr	ป้า
(*younger sister of father*)	ar	อา
(*younger sister of mother*)	nár	น้า
author	nák kǐan	นักเขียน
automatic	àt-Ta-noh-mát	อัตโนมัติ
to avoid	lèek-lîang	หลีกเลี่ยง
awake	Tèurn	ตื่น
awful	yâir mârk	แย่มาก

B

baby	dèhk òrn	เด็กอ่อน
back (*rear*)	kârng lǎng	ข้างหลัง
bad	mâi dee, layw	ไม่ดี เลว
bag, baggage	gra-Pǎo	กระเป๋า
balcony	ra-biang	ระเบียง
bald	hǔa lárn	หัวล้าน
ballpoint pen	Pàrk-gar lôok-lêurn	ปากกาลูกลื่น
bandage	pâr pan plǎir	ผ้าพันแผล
bank	ta-nar-karn	ธนาคาร
bar	bar	บาร์
barber	chârng Tàt pǒm	ช่างตัดผม

to bargain	Tòr rar-kar	ต่อราคา
basement	chán Tâi din	ชั้นใต้ดิน
basket	gra-jàrt, Tra-gâr	กระจาด ตระกร้า
bath	àrng àrp-nárm	อ่างอาบน้ำ
to have a bath	àrp-nárm	อาบน้ำ
bathroom	hôrng nárm	ห้องน้ำ
battery	bàirt-Ter-rêe	แบตเตอรี่
bay	ào	อ่าว
to be	Pehn (*see Basic Grammar*)	เป็น
beach	chai hàrt	ชายหาด
beans	tùa	ถั่ว
beard	kraò	เครา
beautiful	sǔay	สวย
because	pró-wâr	เพราะว่า
bed	Tiang	เตียง
bedroom	hôrng norn	ห้องนอน
bee	pêuhng	ผึ้ง
before	gòrn	ก่อน
to begin	rêrm-Tôn	เริ่มต้น
behind	kârng lǎng	ข้างหลัง
to believe	chêua	เชื่อ
bell	rá-kang	ระฆัง
(*front door*)	gra-dìng	กระดิ่ง
to belong to	Pehn kǒrng	เป็นของ
below	kârng Tâi	ข้างใต้
belt	kěhm-kàt	เข็มขัด
bend (*adj*)	kóhng	โค้ง
(*section of road*)	tarng kóhng	ทางโค้ง
beside	kârng-kârng	ข้าง ๆ
besides	nôrk-jàrk	นอกจาก
best	dee têe-sùt	ดีที่สุด

better	dee gwàr	ดีกว่า
between	rá-wàrng	ระหว่าง
bicycle	jàk-gra-yarn	จักรยาน
big	yài	ใหญ่
bill	bin/bai sèht (interchangeable)	บิล /ใบเสร็จ
bin	tăng ka-yà	ถังขยะ
binoculars	glôrng sòrng tarng glai	กล้องส่องทางไกล
bird	nók	นก
birthday	wan gèrt	วันเกิด
bit, a bit	nít-nòy	นิดหน่อย
to bite	gàt	กัด
blanket	pâr hòm	ผ้าห่ม
to bleed	lêuart òrk	เลือดออก
blind	Tar bòrt	ตาบอด
blister	plăir porng	แผลพอง
blocked	Tan	ตัน
blonde	pŏm sĕe torng	ผมสีทอง
blood	lêuart	เลือด
blouse	sêuar pôo-yĭng	เสื้อผู้หญิง
to blow	Pào	เป่า
to blow-dry (hairdressing)	Pào dai	เป่าไ
boat	reuar	เรือ
body	rârng-gai	ร่างกาย
to boil	Tôm	ต้ม
bomb	lôok rá-bèrt	ลูกระเบิด
bone	gra-dòok	กระดูก
fish bone	gârng Plar	ก้างปลา
book	năng-sĕur	หนังสือ
boot (car)	gra-Prohng tái rót	กระโปรงท้ายรถ
border	chai-dairn	ชายแดน

bored, boring	nâr bèuar	น่าเบื่อ
boss	jâo nai	เจ้านาย
both	táng kôo	ทั้งคู่
bottle	kùat	ขวด
bottle opener	têe Pèrt kùat	ที่เปิดขวด
bottom	gôn	ก้น
bowl	charm	ชาม
box	glòrng	กล่อง
boy	dèhk pôo-chai	เด็กผู้ชาย
boyfriend	fairn	แฟน
bra	sêuar yók song	เสื้อยกทรง
bracelet	gam-lai meur	กำไลมือ
brain	sa-mŏrng	สมอง
brake	bràyk	เบรค
branch (*bank, etc.*)	săr-kăr	สาขา
(*tree*)	gìng-mái	กิ่งไม้
brand	yêe-hôr	ยี่ห้อ
bread	ka-nŏm-Pang	ขนมปัง
to break, broken	Tàirk, hàk	แตก หัก
breakdown	sĭa	เสีย
breakfast	ar-hărn cháo	อาหารเช้า
to breathe	hăi-jai	หายใจ
bridge	sa-parn	สะพาน
briefcase	gra-Păo	กระเป๋า
to bring	ao mar	เอามา
broad	gwârng	กว้าง
brooch	kĕhm glàt-sêuar	เข็มกลัดเสื้อ
brother (*older*)	pêe chai	พี่ชาย
(*younger*)	nórng chai	น้องชาย
brother-in-law (*older*)	pêe kŏei	พี่เขย
(*younger*)	nórng kŏei	น้องเขย

bruise	ta-lòrk	ถลอก
bucket	tăng	ถัง
Buddha	prá-pút-ta-jâo	พระพุทธเจ้า
Buddhism	sàrt-sa-năr pút	ศาสนาพุทธ
buffet	búf-fây	บุฟเฟ่ต์
to build	sârng	สร้าง
building	ar-karn/Tèuhk (interchangeable)	อาคาร/ตึก
bulb (light)	lòrt fai	หลอดไฟ
to bump	chon	ชน
bumper	gan-chon	กันชน
bungalow	bang-ga-loh	บังกะโล
to burn	mâi	ไหม้
bus	rót may	รถเมล์
business	tú-rá	ธุระ
businessman/woman	nák tú-rá-gìt	นักธุรกิจ
busy	yûng	ยุ่ง
but	Tàir	แต่
butterfly	pěe-sêuar	ผีเสื้อ
button	gra-dum	กระดุม
to buy	séur	ซื้อ
by	dohy	โดย

C

cake	ka-nŏm káyk	ขนมเค้ก
calculator	krêuarng kít lâyk	เครื่องคิดเลข
calendar	Pa-Ti-tin	ปฏิทิน
to call	rîak	เรียก
(telephone)	toh	โทร.
calm	sa-ngòp	สงบ
camcorder	glôrng vee-dee-oh	กล้องวิดีโอ

camera	glôrng tài rôop	กล้องถ่ายรูป
can (*to be able*)	tam dâi	ทำได้
can (*tin*)	gra-Pŏrng	กระป๋อง
can opener	têe Pèrt gra-Pŏrng	ที่เปิดกระป๋อง
canal	klorng	คลอง
to cancel	yók-lêrk	ยกเลิก
candle	tian-kăi	เทียนไข
car	rót yon	รถยนต์
car park	têe jòrt rót	ที่จอดรถ
careful	rá-wang	ระวัง
carpet	prom	พรม
carriage (*train*)	boh-gêe	โบกี้
carrier bag	tŭng sài kŏrng	ถุงใส่ของ
to carry	tĕur	ถือ
cash	ngern sòt	เงินสด
cassette	táyp kárt-sèht	เทปคาสเส็ท
cassette player	krêuarng-lêhn táyp kárt-sèht	เครื่องเล่นเทปคาสเส็ท
cat	mairw	แมว
to catch	jàp	จับ
cave	tâm	ถ้ำ
cemetery	sù-sărn/Pàr-chár (*interchangeable*)	สุสาน/ ปาช้า
central	Trong glarng	ตรงกลาง
centre	sŏon glarng	ศูนย์กลาง
certain	nâir-norn	แน่นอน
certificate	bai ráp-rorng	ใบรับรอง
chain	sôh	โซ่
chair	gâo-êe	เก้าอี้
to change	Plìan	เปลี่ยน
change (*coins*)	sàyt sa-Tarng	เศษสตางค์

cheap	tòok	ถูก
to check	chéhk doo	เช็คดู
cheese	noei kǎihng	เนยแข็ง
cheque	chéhk	เช็ค
chewing gum	màrk fa-ràng	หมากฝรั่ง
chicken	gài	ไก่
child, children	dèhk	เด็ก
chilli	prík	พริก
chocolate	chók-goh-láiht	ช็อคโกแลต
to choose	lêuark	เลือก
Christ, Jesus Christ	prá yay-soo	พระเยซู
church	bòht	โบสถ์
cigar	sí-gâr	ซิก้าร์
cigarette	bu-rèe	บุหรี่
cinema	rohng-nǎng	โรงหนัง
circle	wong glom	วงกลม
city	meuarng	เมือง
city centre	jài-glarng meuarng	ใจกลางเมือง
class	chán	ชั้น
to clean	tam kwarm sa-àrt	ทำความสะอาด
clean	sa-àrt	สะอาด
clear *(transparent)*	sǎi	ใส
(unmistakable)	chát jayn	ชัดเจน
clever	cha-làrt	ฉลาด
cliff	nâr-pǎr	หน้าผา
to climb	Peen	ปีน
clinic	klee-nìk	คลีนิค
clock	nar-lí-gar	นาฬิกา
to close, closed	Pìt	ปิด
close by, close to	glâi	ใกล้
cloth	pâr	ผ้า

clothes	sêuar pâr	เสื้อผ้า
clothes peg	mái nèep	ไม้หนีบ
cloud	mâyk	เมฆ
cloudy	mâyk kréuhm	เมฆครึ้ม
coast	chai fàng	ชายฝั่ง
coathanger	mái kwǎirn sêuar	ไม้แขวนเสื้อ
cockroach	ma-lairng sàrp	แมลงสาบ
coconut milk	ga-tí	กะทิ
code (telephone, etc.)	rá-hàt	รหัส
coffee	gar-fair	กาแฟ
coin	rǐan	เหรียญ
cold	nǎo	หนาว
to have a cold	Pehn wàt	เป็นหวัด
collar (shirt)	kor sêuar	คอเสื้อ
to collect (objects, etc.)	sà-sǒm	สะสม
college	wít-ta-yar-lai	วิทยาลัย
colour	sěe	สี
colour blind	Tar bòrt sěe	ตาบอดสี
colour film	feem sěe	ฟิล์มสี
to comb, comb	wěe	หวี
to come	mar	มา
to come back	glàp mar	กลับมา
to come in	kâo mar	เข้ามา
comfortable	sa-bai	สบาย
company (firm)	bor-ri-sàt	บริษัท
to compare	Prìap-tîap	เปรียบเทียบ
compass	kěhm-tít	เข็มทิศ
to complain (express discontent)	bòn	บ่น
(make a charge)	rórng-rian	ร้องเรียน
condom	tǔng-yarng	ถุงยาง

to confirm	yeurn-yan	ยืนยัน
conscious	róo-sèuhk Tua	รู้สึกตัว
consulate	sa-tǎrn gong-sǔn	สถานกงศุล
contact lens	korn-tàihk lehn	คอนแท็คเลนส์
contraceptive pill	yar kum gam-nèrt	ยาคุมกำเนิด
contract	sǎn-yar	สัญญา
to cook	tam ar-hǎrn	ทำอาหาร
cook (*person*)	pôr krua (m)	พ่อครัว
	mâir krua (f)	แม่ครัว
cooker	Tao	เตา
cool	yehn	เย็น
copper	torng dairng	ทองแดง
copy (*duplicate*)	sǎm-nao	สำเนา
corner	hǔa mum	หัวมุม
correct	tòok-Tôrng	ถูกต้อง
corridor	tarng dern	ทางเดิน
cosmetics	krêuarng sǎm-arng	เครื่องสำอางค์
cost	rar-kar	ราคา
cotton	pâr fâi	ผ้าฝ้าย
cotton wool	sǎm-lee	สำลี
to cough	ai	ไอ
to count	náp	นับ
counter	káo-Têr	เค้าน์เตอร์
country (*nation*)	Pra-tâyt	ประเทศ
countryside	chon-na-bòt	ชนบท
cow	wua	วัว
crate	lang	ลัง
cream	kreem	ครีม
to cross over	kârm	ข้าม
crowded	kon nâihn	คนแน่น
to cry (*scream*)	rórng	ร้อง

(weep)	rórng hâi	ร้องไห้
cup	tûay	ถ้วย
cupboard	Tôo	ตู้
to cure	rák-sǎr	รักษา
curly (*hair*)	pǒm-yìk	ผมหยิก
curtain	mârn	ม่าน
custom	Pra-pay-nee	ประเพณี
customs	sǔn-la-gar-gorn	ศุลกากร
to cut	Tàt	ตัด
cyclist	kon tèep jàk-gra-yarn	คนถีบจักรยาน

D

daily	rai wan	รายวัน
to damage	tam kwarm sǐa-hǎi	ทำความเสียหาย
damage	kâr sǐa-hǎi	ค่าเสียหาย
to dance	Têhn ram	เต้นรำ
danger, dangerous	an-Ta-rai	อันตราย
dark (*devoid of light*)	mêurt	มืด
darling	têe rák	ที่รัก
date (*day*)	wan têe	วันที่
daughter	lôok sǎo	ลูกสาว
daughter-in-law	lôok sa-pái	ลูกสะใภ้
day	wan	วัน
dead, death	Tai	ตาย
deaf	hǒo nùak	หูหนวก
to decide	Tàt-sǐn-jai	ตัดสินใจ
deep	léuhk	ลึก
defect, defective	cham-rút	ชำรุด
definitely	nâir-norn	แน่นอน
degree (*temperature*)	ong-sǎr	องศา

delay (*train, etc.*)	sĭa way-lar	เสียเวลา
delicious	a-ròy	อร่อย
to deliver	sòng	ส่ง
dentist	mŏr fan	หมอฟัน
denture	fan Plorm	ฟันปลอม
deodorant	yar dàp glîn Tua	ยาดับกลิ่นตัว
to depart	òrk dern tarng	ออกเดินทาง
department (*office*)	pa-nàirk	แผนก
department store	hârng sàp-pa-sĭn-kár	ห้างสรรพสินค้า
deposit	ngern mát-jam	เงินมัดจำ
dessert	kŏrng wărn	ของหวาน
destination (*travel*)	Plai tarng	ปลายทาง
detail	rai la-ìat	รายละเอียด
to develop	pát-ta-nar	พัฒนา
dialling code	rá-hàt toh-ra-sàp	รหัสโทรศัพท์
diamond	péht	เพชร
diary	sa-mùt ban-téuhk	สมุดบันทึก
dictionary	pót-ja-nar-nú-grom	พจนานุกรม
to die	Tai	ตาย
diesel	dee-sayn	ดีเซล
different	Tàirk-Tàrng	แตกต่าง
difficult	yârk	ยาก
dining room	hôrng gin kâo	ห้องกินข้าว
dinner	ar-hărn yehn	อาหารเย็น
direct	Trong	ตรง
direction	sâyn tarng	เส้นทาง
dirty	sòk-ga-Pròk	สกปรก
disabled	pí-garn	พิการ
disappointed	pìt wăng	ผิดหวัง
dislocated (*joint*)	klêuarn	เคลื่อน
distance	rá-yá tarng	ระยะทาง

distilled water	nárm glàn	น้ำกลั่น
to dive (scuba dive)	dam nárm	ดำน้ำ
divorced	yàr	หย่า
dizzy	wian hǔa	เวียนหัว
to do	tam	ทำ
doctor	mǒr	หมอ
dog	mǎr	หมา
doll	Túk-ga-Tar	ตุ๊กตา
door	Pra-Too	ประตู
double	sǒrng tâo	สองเท่า
downstairs	chán lârng	ชั้นล่าง
to dream	fǎn	ฝัน
to dress	Tàirng Tua	แต่งตัว
dress	krêuarng Tàirng Tua	เครื่องแต่งตัว
to drink	dèurm	ดื่ม
drink	krêuarng dèurm	เครื่องดื่ม
drinking water	nárm dèurm	น้ำดื่ม
to drive (car)	kàp	ขับ
driver	kon kàp	คนขับ
driving licence	bai kàp kèe	ใบขับขี่
to drown	jom nárm Tai	จมน้ำตาย
drug	yar	ยา
drugs	yar sàyp Tìt	ยาเสพติด
drunk	mao lâo	เมาเหล้า
dry	hâirng	แห้ง
during	rá-wàrng	ระหว่าง
dust	fùn	ฝุ่น
dustbin	tǎng ka-yà	ถังขยะ

149

E

each *(per person)*	kon lá	คนละ
(per piece)	an lá	อันละ
early	gòrn way-lar	ก่อนเวลา
earring	Tûm hǒo	ตุ้มหู
earth *(world)*	lôhk	โลก
east	tít Ta-wan òrk	ทิศตะวันออก
easy	ngâi	ง่าย
to eat	gin	กิน
egg	kài	ไข่
either	an-dai-an-nèuhng	อันใดอันหนึ่ง
either … or …	rěur	หรือ
elastic	sǎi yarng yêurt	สายยางยืด
elastic band	nǎng sa-Tík	หนังสะติ๊ก
electricity	fai-fár	ไฟฟ้า
electronic	ee-léhk-troh-nìk	อิเล็คโทรนิกส์
elephant	chárng	ช้าง
else	èek	อีก
embassy	sa-tǎrn tôot	สถานทูต
emergency	chùk-chěrn	ฉุกเฉิน
to empty	tay òrk	เทออก
empty *(vacant)*	wârng	ว่าง
(bottle, etc.)	Plào	เปล่า
to end	sîn-sùt	สิ้นสุด
end *(termination)*	jòp	จบ
(tip)	Plai	ปลาย
engaged *(to be married)*	mân	หมั้น
(occupied, telephone)	mâi wârng	ไม่ว่าง
engine	krêuarng yon	เครื่องยนต์
England	Pra-tâyt ang-grìt	ประเทศอังกฤษ

English (*person*)	kon ang-grìt	คนอังกฤษ
(*language*)	par-săr ang-grìt	ภาษาอังกฤษ
to enjoy	sa-nùk	สนุก
enough	por	พอ
to enter	kâo	เข้า
entrance	tarng kâo	ทางเข้า
envelope	sorng jòt-măi	ซองจดหมาย
to envy	ìt-chăr	อิจฉา
equal	tâo-gan	เท่ากัน
escalator	ban-dai lêuarn	บันไดเลื่อน
especially	dohy cha-pó	โดยเฉพาะ
essential	sìng jam-Pehn	สิ่งจำเป็น
even (*number*)	lâyk kôo	เลขคู่
evening	Torn kâm	ตอนค่ำ
everyone	túk kon	ทุกคน
everything	túk yàrng	ทุกอย่าง
everywhere	túk têe	ทุกที่
example	Tua-yàrng	ตัวอย่าง
excellent	yôrt-yîam	ยอดเยี่ยม
except	yók-wáyn	ยกเว้น
to exchange (*money*)	lâirk ngern	แลกเงิน
exchange rate	àt-Trar lâirk-Plìan	อัตราแลกเปลี่ยน
excited, exciting	Tèurn-Têhn	ตื่นเต้น
Excuse me	kŏr tôht	ขอโทษ
exhibition	ngarn sa-dairng/ní-tát-sa-garn (*interchangeable*)	งานแสดง/นิทรรศการ
exit	tarng òrk	ทางออก
to expect	kârt wăng	คาดหวัง
expensive	pairng	แพง
to explain	a-tí-bai	อธิบาย
to export	sòng òrk	ส่งออก

| express | dùan | ด่วน |
| extra | pí-sàyt | พิเศษ |

F

face	bai nâr	ใบหน้า
facsimile, fax	fàihk	แฟกส์
factory	rohng-ngarn	โรงงาน
to faint	Pehn lom	เป็นลม
fake	kŏrng Plorm	ของปลอม
to fall (*down/over*)	hòk lóm	หกล้ม
false	pìt	ผิด
family	krôrp-krua	ครอบครัว
famous	mee chêur-sĭang	มีชื่อเสียง
fan (*air*)	pát-lom	พัดลม
far	glai	ไกล
farmer	chao nar	ชาวนา
fashion	fair-chân	แฟชั่น
fast	rehw	เร็ว
fat (*adj*)	ûan	อ้วน
father	pôr	พ่อ
father-in-law (*groom's*)	pôr sǎr-mee/	พ่อสามี/
	pôr pǔa (*casual word*)	พ่อผัว
(*bride's*)	pôr Tar	พ่อตา
fee	kâr tam-niam	ค่าธรรมเนียม
to feel	róo-sèuhk	รู้สึก
to feel ill	mâi sa-bai	ไม่สบาย
to feel well	sa-bai dee	สบายดี
female	pôo-yĭng	ผู้หญิง
fence	rúa	รั้ว
ferry	reuar kârm fârk	เรือข้ามฟาก

festival	tâyt-sa-garn	เทศกาล
fever	Pehn kâi	เป็นไข้
(a) few	léhk nóy	เล็กน้อย
fiancé(e)	kôo mân	คู่หมั้น
field	tûng nar	ทุ่งนา
to fight	Tòr-sôo	ต่อสู้
file (documents)	fáirm	แฟ้ม
to fill	Term	เติม
film (cinema)	năng	หนัง
(camera)	feem	ฟิล์ม
filter (n)	krêuarng grorng	เครื่องกรอง
to find	jer	เจอ
fine (OK)	oh-kay	โอเค
(penalty)	kâr Pràp	ค่าปรับ
(weather)	dee	ดี
to finish	sèht	เสร็จ
fire brigade	nùay dàp plerng	หน่วยดับเพลิง
fire extinguisher	krêuarng dàp plerng	เครื่องดับเพลิง
firm (certain)	nâir norn	แน่นอน
first	râirk/têe nèuhng (interchangeable)	แรก/ ที่หนึ่ง
first-aid kit	krêuarng Pa-tŏm pa-yar-barn	เครื่องปฐมพยาบาล
fitting room	hôrng lorng sêuar	ห้องลองเสื้อ
fizzy	sâr	ซ่า
flag	tong	ธง
flash (camera)	flâiht	แฟลช
flat (apartment)	flâiht	แฟลต
(battery)	mòt	หมด
(level)	bairn	แบน
flavour	rót chârt	รสชาติ

flea	Tua màt	ตัวหมัด
flight	tîaw bin	เที่ยวบิน
flood	nárm tûam	น้ำท่วม
floor	péurn	พื้น
(storey)	chán	ชั้น
flower	dòrk mái	ดอกไม้
fluid	kŏrng lăyw	ของเหลว
to fly	bin	บิน
fly (insect)	ma-lairng wan	แมลงวัน
fog	mòrk	หมอก
foggy	mòrk jàt	หมอกจัด
folk music	don-Tree péurn-meuarng	ดนตรีพื้นเมือง
to follow	Tìt-Tarm	ติดตาม
food	ar-hărn	อาหาร
footpath	tarng táo	ทางเท้า
for	săm-ràp	สำหรับ
forbidden	hârm	ห้าม
foreigner	chao Tàrng Pra-tâyt	ชาวต่างประเทศ
forest	Pàr mái	ป่าไม้
forever	Ta-lòrt Pai	ตลอดไป
to forget	leurm	ลืม
to forgive	hâi a-pai	ให้อภัย
fork	sôrm	ส้อม
form	bàirp form	แบบฟอร์ม
fortnight	sŏrng ar-tít	สองอาทิตย์
fountain	nárm-pú	น้ำพุ
fracture	roy Tàirk	รอยแตก
freckle	Tòk grà	ตกกระ
to free	Plòy	ปล่อย
free (gratis)	free	ฟรี
frequent	bòy	บ่อย

fresh	sòt	สด
fridge	Tôo yehn	ตู้เย็น
friend	pêuarn	เพื่อน
friendly	Pehn mít	เป็นมิตร
frightened	glua	กลัว
frog	gòp	กบ
from	jàrk	จาก
front	kârng nâr	ข้างหน้า
frontier	chai dairn	ชายแดน
fruit	pǒn-la-mái	ผลไม้
to fry (*deep-fry*)	tôrt	ทอด
(*stir-fry*)	pàt	ผัด
frying pan	gra-tá	กระทะ
full	Tehm	เต็ม
full up	ìm	อิ่ม
funeral	ngarn sòp	งานศพ
funny (*amusing*)	Ta-lòk	ตลก
(*peculiar*)	Plàirk	แปลก
fuse (*in plug*)	fiw	ฟิวส์

G

garden	sǔan	สวน
garlic	gra-tiam	กระเทียม
gas	gáirt	แก๊ส
gate	Pra-Too	ประตู
(*airport*)	tarng òrk	ทางออก
gay (*homosexual*)	gay, gra-toei	เกย์ กระเทย
general	tûa Pai	ทั่วไป
generous	jai gwârng	ใจกว้าง
gentle	su-pârp	สุภาพ

155

gents	hôrng nárm chai	ห้องน้ำชาย
genuine	kŏrng táir	ของแท้
germ	chéuar rôhk	เชื้อโรค
to get off (*bus, etc*)	long	ลง
to get on (*bus, etc*)	kêuhn	ขึ้น
to get up	Tèurn	ตื่น
gift	kŏrng-kwăn	ของขวัญ
girl	dèhk pôo-yĭng	เด็กผู้หญิง
girlfriend	fairn	แฟน
to give	hâi	ให้
glad	yin-dee	ยินดี
glass	gâirw	แก้ว
glasses (*spectacles*)	wâirn-Tar	แว่นตา
glue	gao	กาว
to go	Pai	ไป
God	prá-Pehn-jâo	พระเป็นเจ้า
gold	torng	ทอง
golf	górp	กอล์ฟ
golf clubs	mái górp	ไม้กอล์ฟ
golf course	sa-nărm górp	สนามกอล์ฟ
good	dee	ดี
goodbye	lar-gòrn	ลาก่อน
goods	sĭn-kár	สินค้า
government	rát-ta-barn	รัฐบาล
grandchild/ren	lărn	หลาน
granddaughter	lărn săo	หลานสาว
grandfather (*paternal*)	Pòo	ปู่
(*maternal*)	Tar	ตา
grandmother (*paternal*)	yâr	ย่า
(*maternal*)	yai	ยาย
grandson	lărn chai	หลานชาย

grass	yâr	หญ้า
greasy	Pehn man	เป็นมัน
Great!	yôrt	ยอด
to grill	yârng	ย่าง
ground	péurn-din	พื้นดิน
ground floor	chán lârng	ชั้นล่าง
group	glùm	กลุ่ม
guarantee	Pra-gan	ประกัน
	gar-ran-Tee *(casual word)*	การันตี
guard *(on train)*	nai Trùat	นายตรวจ
guest house	gáyt-háo	เกสต์เฮ้าส์
guide	mák-kú-tâyt/	มัคคุเทศน์/
	gái *(casual word)*	ไกด์
guidebook	kôo-meur nam tîaw	คู่มือนำเที่ยว
gun	Peurn	ปืน

H

hairdresser	chârng tam pŏm	ช่างทำผม
hairdryer	têe Pào pŏm	ที่เป่าผม
half	krêuhng	ครึ่ง
hammer	kórn	ค้อน
handbag	gra-Păo těur	กระเป๋าถือ
handkerchief	pâr chét nâr	ผ้าเช็ดหน้า
handle	dârm	ด้าม
to hang up *(telephone)*	warng hŏo	วางหู
hangover	mao kárng	เมาค้าง
happy	mee kwarm sùk	มีความสุข
harbour	târ reuar	ท่าเรือ
hard	kăihng	แข็ง
(difficult)	yârk	ยาก
hat	mùak	หมวก

to hate	glìat	เกลียด
to have	mee	มี
he	káo	เขา
headlights	fai nâr rót	ไฟหน้ารถ
headphones	hŏo fang	หูฟัง
healthy	sùk-ka-pârp dee	สุขภาพดี
to hear	dâi yin	ได้ยิน
hearing aid	krêuarng chûay fang	เครื่องช่วยฟัง
heart attack	hŭa-jai wai	หัวใจวาย
heartbroken	òk hàk	อกหัก
heat	kwarm rórn	ความร้อน
heaven	sa-wăn	สวรรค์
heavy	nàk	หนัก
heel (*shoe*)	sôn rorng táo	ส้นรองเท้า
height	kwarm sŏong	ความสูง
hell	na-rók	นรก
hello	sa-wàt-dee	สวัสดี
helmet (*motorcycle*)	mùak gan nók	หมวกกันน็อก
to help	chûay	ช่วย
her (*pron*)	káo	เขา
(*adj*)	kŏrng káo	ของเขา
here	têe nêe	ที่นี่
hers	kŏrng káo	ของเขา
hiccups	sa-èuhk	สะอึก
high	sŏong	สูง
hill	nern/doy (*interchangeable*)	เนิน/ดอย
hill tribe	chao kăo	ชาวเขา
him	káo	เขา
to hire	châo	เช่า
his	kŏrng káo	ของเขา

to hit	Tee	ตี
hobby	ngarn a-di-ràyk	งานอดิเรก
to hold	těur	ถือ
hole	roo	รู
holidays	wan yùt	วันหยุด
(at) home	yòo bârn	อยู่บ้าน
to be homesick	kít-těuhng bârn	คิดถึงบ้าน
honest	sêur-sàt	ซื่อสัตย์
honey	nárm-pêuhng	น้ำผึ้ง
to hope	wăng	หวัง
horrible	yâir mârk	แย่มาก
horse	már	ม้า
hospital	rohng-pa-yar-barn	โรงพยาบาล
hot	rórn	ร้อน
(spicy)	pèht	เผ็ด
hotel	rohng-rairm	โรงแรม
hour	chûa-mohng	ชั่วโมง
house	bârn	บ้าน
how	yàrng-rai	อย่างไร
hungry	hĭw	หิว
hurry	rêep-rórn	รีบร้อน
to hurt: it hurts	jèhp	เจ็บ
husband	săr-mee	สามี
	pŭa (casual word)	ผัว
hut	gra-tôm	กระท่อม

I

I (male)	pŏm	ผม
(female)	di-chán	ดิฉัน
ice	nárm-kăihng	น้ำแข็ง

ice cream	ai-sa-kreem	ไอศกรีม
idea	kwarm kít	ความคิด
if	târ	ถ้า
ill	mâi sa-bai	ไม่สบาย
immediately	tan-tee	ทันที
impatient	jai rórn	ใจร้อน
to import	nam kâo	นำเข้า
important	sǎm-kan	สำคัญ
impossible	Pehn Pai mâi dâi	เป็นไปไม่ได้
in	nai	ใน
included, inclusive	ruam mòt	รวมหมด
indoors	nai rôm	ในร่ม
industry	ùt-sǎr-ha-gam	อุตสาหกรรม
infected	Tìt chéuar	ติดเชื้อ
infection	àk-sàyp	อักเสบ
informal	lam-lorng	ลำลอง
information	kào sǎrn	ข่าวสาร
injection	chèet yar	ฉีดยา
to injure	bàrt-jèhp	บาดเจ็บ
ink	mèuhk	หมึก
innocent	bor-ri-sùt	บริสุทธิ์
insect	ma-lairng	แมลง
inside	kârng nai	ข้างใน
instant coffee	gar-fair sǎm-rèht-rôop	กาแฟสำเร็จรูป
instead of	tairn têe	แทนที่
to insult	doo-tòok	ดูถูก
insurance, to insure	Pra-gan	ประกัน
insurance certificate	grom-ma-tan Pra-gan pai	กรมธรรม์ประกันภัย
intelligent	cha-làrt	ฉลาด
interested	sǒn-jai	สนใจ
interesting	nâr sǒn-jai	น่าสนใจ

interior	pai nai	ภายใน
international	rá-wàrng Pra-tâyt	ระหว่างประเทศ
to interpret	Plair	แปล
interpreter	lârm	ล่าม
interview (*police*)	sòrp Pàrk-kam	สอบปากคำ
into	kâo kârng nai	เข้าข้างใน
to iron	rêet pâr	รีดผ้า
iron (*for clothes*)	Tao-rêet	เตารีด
(*metal*)	lèhk	เหล็ก
island	gò	เกาะ
it	man	มัน
itchy	kan	คัน
its	kŏrng man	ของมัน

J

jack (*for car*)	mâir-rairng	แม่แรง
jacket	sêuar nôrk	เสื้อนอก
jar	gra-pùk, lŏh	กระปุก โหล
jeans	yeen	ยีนส์
jelly	yehn-lêe	เยลลี่
jellyfish	mairng ga-prun	แมงกะพรุน
jetty	târ reuar	ท่าเรือ
job	ngarn	งาน
joke	rêuarng Ta-lòk	เรื่องตลก
journalist	nák kào	นักข่าว
journey	garn dern tarng	การเดินทาง
judge	pôo-pí-pârk-săr	ผู้พิพากษา
	sărn (*casual word*)	ศาล
jug	yèuark	เหยือก
(fruit) juice	nárm pón-la-mái	น้ำผลไม้

to jump	gra-dòht	กระโดด
to jump the queue	lát kiw	ลัดคิว
junction	tarng yâirk	ทางแยก
just (only)	tâo nán	เท่านั้น

K

to keep	gèhp	เก็บ
kettle	gar Tôm nárm	กาต้มน้ำ
key	gun-jair	กุญแจ
keyring	puang gun-jair	พวงกุญแจ
to kill	kâr	ฆ่า
kilo(gram)	gi-loh	กิโล
kilometre	gi-loh-máyt	กิโลเมตร
kind (sort)	cha-nít	ชนิด
(generous)	jai dee	ใจดี
king	ga-sàt	กษัตริย์
to kiss	jòop	จูบ
kitchen	krua	ครัว
knickers	garng-gayng-nai	กางเกงใน
knife	mêet	มีด
to knock	kó	เคาะ
to know	róo-jàk	รู้จัก

L

label	cha-làrk	ฉลาก
ladder	gra-dai	กระได
ladies (toilets)	hôrng nárm yǐng	ห้องน้ำหญิง
lamb	gàih	แกะ
lamp	kohm-fai	โคมไฟ
lamppost	sǎo fai	เสาไฟ

land	têe din	ที่ดิน
language	par-săr	ภาษา
large	yài	ใหญ่
last *(final)*	sùt-tái	สุดท้าย
(previous)	têe láirw	ที่แล้ว
late *(nighttime)*	dèuhk	ดึก
(train, etc.)	mar chár	มาช้า
later	tee lăng	ทีหลัง
to laugh	hŭa-ró	หัวเราะ
law	gòt-măi	กฎหมาย
lawyer	ta-nai kwarm	ทนายความ
lazy	kêe-giat	ขี้เกียจ
lead	Ta-gùa	ตะกั่ว
leaf	bai mái	ใบไม้
leaflet	bai Pliw	ใบปลิว
to learn	rian róo	เรียนรู้
lease	săn-yar châo	สัญญาเช่า
least: at least	yàrng nóy têe sùt	อย่างน้อยที่สุด
to leave *(message)*	sàng kôr-kwarm	สั่งข้อความ
(go away)	Pai	ไป
left	sái, tarng sái	ซ้าย ทางซ้าย
left-handed	ta-nàt sái	ถนัดซ้าย
left luggage	têe fàrk gra-Păo	ที่ฝากกระเป๋า
lemon	ma-nao	มะนาว
to lend	hâi yeurm	ให้ยืม
length	kwarm yao	ความยาว
lens	lehn	เลนส์
less	nóy	น้อย
to let *(allow)*	Plòy	ปล่อย
(rent)	hâi châo	ให้เช่า
letter	jòt-măi	จดหมาย

letterbox	Tôo jòt-măi	ตู้จดหมาย
lettuce	pàk-gàrt	ผักกาด
library	hôrng sa-mùt	ห้องสมุด
licence	bai a-nú-yârt	ใบอนุญาต
lid	făr	ฝา
to lie	goh-hòk	โกหก
to lie down	norn long	นอนลง
life	chee-wít	ชีวิต
lifejacket	sêuar choo-chêep	เสื้อชูชีพ
lift	líf	ลิฟต์
to light (*fire*)	jùt fai	จุดไฟ
light (*ray*)	săirng sa-wàrng	แสงสว่าง
(*weight*)	bao	เบา
lighter (*cigarette*)	fai cháihk	ไฟแช็ก
lightning	fár pàr	ฟ้าผ่า
to like	chôrp	ชอบ
like (*similar*)	mĕuarn	เหมือน
lion	sĭng-Toh	สิงห์โต
lipstick	líp-sa-Tĭk	ลิปสติก
liquid	kŏrng lăyw	ของเหลว
list	ban-chee rai-chêur	บัญชีรายชื่อ
to listen	fang	ฟัง
litre	lít	ลิตร
litter	ka-yà	ขยะ
little	léhk	เล็ก
(a) little	léhk nóy	เล็กน้อย
to lock (*door, etc.*)	lók	ล็อค
long	yao	ยาว
to look (*see*)	morng	มอง
lorry	rót ban-túk	รถบรรทุก
to lose	tam hăi	ทำหาย

lottery	lót-Ter-rêe	ล็อตเตอรี่
loud	dang	ดัง
to love	rák	รัก
low	Tàm	ต่ำ
lucky	chôhk dee	โชคดี
luggage	gra-Pǎo	กระเป๋า
lunch	ar-hǎrn glarng-wan	อาหารกลางวัน

M

machine	krêuarng jàk	เครื่องจักร
mad	bâr	บ้า
magazine	nít-Ta-yá-sǎrn	นิตยสาร
mail	jòt-mǎi	จดหมาย
to make	tam	ทำ
make-up	krêuarng sǎm-arng	เครื่องสำอางค์
male, man	pôo-chai	ผู้ชาย
manager	pôo-jàt-garn	ผู้จัดการ
many	mârk-mai	มากมาย
not many	mâi mârk tâo-rài	ไม่มากเท่าไหร่
map	pǎirn-têe	แผนที่
marble	hǐn-òrn	หินอ่อน
market	Ta-làrt	ตลาด
married	Tàirng-ngarn láirw	แต่งงานแล้ว
massage	nûat	นวด
matches (cigar, etc.)	mái kèt	ไม้ขีด
material (cloth)	pâr	ผ้า
matter: it doesn't matter	mâi Pehn rai	ไม่เป็นไร
what's the matter?	gèrt a-rai kêuhn	เกิดอะไรขึ้น
me (male)	pǒm	ผม
(female)	di-chán	ดิฉัน

to mean	mǎi kwarm wâr	หมายความว่า
to measure	wát	วัด
meat	néuar sàt	เนื้อสัตว์
medicine	yar	ยา
to meet	póp	พบ
meeting (*business*)	Pra-chum	ประชุม
member	sa-mar-chík	สมาชิก
menu	may-noo	เมนู
message	kôr-kwarm	ข้อความ
metal	loh-hà	โลหะ
meter	mí-Têr	มิเตอร์
metre	máyt	เมตร
midday	tîang wan	เที่ยงวัน
middle	Trong glarng	ตรงกลาง
middle-aged	wai glarng kon	วัยกลางคน
midnight	tîang keurn	เที่ยงคืน
mile	mai	ไมล์
milk	nom	นม
mine (*of me*)	kôrng pǒm/di-chán	ของผม/ดิฉัน
mineral water	nárm râir	น้ำแร่
ministry	gra-suang	กระทรวง
minute (*time*)	nar-tee	นาที
mirror	gra-jòk	กระจก
to miss (*bus, etc.*)	plârt	พลาด
(*nostalgia*)	kít-těuhng	คิดถึง
Miss	narng-sǎo	นางสาว
mistake	kwarm pìt-plârt	ความผิดพลาด
mixed	pa-sǒm	ผสม
modern	tan sa-mǎi	ทันสมัย
money	ngern	เงิน
month	deuarn	เดือน

monthly	rai deuarn	รายเดือน
monument	a-nú-săr-wa-ree	อนุสาวรีย์
moon	prá-jan	พระจันทร์
more	gwàr	กว่า
no more	por láirw	พอแล้ว
morning	cháo	เช้า
mosquito	yung	ยุง
mosquito net	múng	มุ้ง
most	sùan yài	ส่วนใหญ่
mother	mâir	แม่
mother-in-law (*bride's*)	mâir yai	แม่ยาย
(*groom's*)	mâir săr-mee	แม่สามี
	mâir pŭa (*casual word*)	แม่ผัว
motorcycle	rót mor-Ter-sai	รถมอร์เตอร์ไซค์
motorway	tarng lŭang	ทางหลวง
mountain	poo kăo	ภูเขา
moustache	nùat	หนวด
Mr	nai	นาย
Mrs	narng	นาง
much	mârk	มาก
museum	pí-pít-ta-pan	พิพิธภัณฑ์
mushroom	hèht	เห็ด
music	don-Tree	ดนตรี
must	Tôrng	ต้อง
my	kŏrng pŏm/di-chán	ของผม/ดิฉัน

nail (*DIY*)	Ta-Poo	ตะปู
(*finger*)	léhp meur	เล็บมือ
(*toe*)	léhp táo	เล็บเท้า

nail clippers	têe Tàt léhp	ที่ตัดเล็บ
naked	lôn-jôn	ล่อนจ้อน
name	chêur	ชื่อ
napkin (for dining)	pâr chét Pàrk	ผ้าเช็ดปาก
narrow	kâirp	แคบ
nationality	săn-chârt	สัญชาติ
near, nearby	glâi	ใกล้
necessary	jam-Pehn	จำเป็น
necklace	sôy kor	สร้อยคอ
to need	Tôrng-garn	ต้องการ
needle	kěhm	เข็ม
nephew	lărn chai	หลานชาย
never	mâi koei	ไม่เคย
new	mài	ใหม่
New Year	Pee mài	ปีใหม่
news	kào	ข่าว
newspaper	năng-sěur pim	หนังสือพิมพ์
next	Tòr-Pai	ต่อไป
nice (person, weather)	dee	ดี
niece	lărn săo	หลานสาว
night	glarng keurn	กลางคืน
nightclub	nái-klàp	ไนท์คลับ
no	mâi	ไม่
noisy	nùak hŏo	หนวกหู
noodles	gŭay-tĭaw	ก๋วยเตี๋ยว
north	tít nĕuar	ทิศเหนือ
nosebleed	lêuart gam-dao òrk	เลือดกำเดาออก
not	mâi	ไม่
nothing	mâi mee a-rai	ไม่มีอะไร
now	dĭaw née	เดี๋ยวนี้
number (figure)	măi lâyk	หมายเลข

(*hotel room, etc.*)	ber hôrng	เบอร์ห้อง
(*telephone*)	ber toh-ra-sàp	เบอร์โทรศัพท์
nurse	pa-yar-barn	พยาบาล
nylon	nai-lôn	ไนล่อน

O

occasionally	barng-kráng barng-krao	บางครั้งบางคราว
occupied (*seat*)	jorng láirw	จองแล้ว
odd (*strange*)	Plàirk	แปลก
(*number*)	lâyk kêe	เลขคี่
of	kŏrng	ของ
to offer	sa-něr	เสนอ
office	têe tam ngarn	ที่ทำงาน
often	bòy-bòy	บ่อย ๆ
OK	oh-kay	โอเค
old (*people*)	gàir	แก่
(*things*)	gào	เก่า
old-fashioned	lár sa-măi	ล้าสมัย
on	bon	บน
onion	hŭa hŏrm	หัวหอม
only	tâo-nán	เท่านั้น
to open, opened	Pèrt	เปิด
operation (*medical*)	pàr-Tàt	ผ่าตัด
opposite	Trong kârm	ตรงข้าม
or	rĕur	หรือ
to order	sàng	สั่ง
other	an èurn	อันอื่น
our, ours	kŏrng rao	ของเรา
out (*not in*)	mâi yòo	ไม่อยู่
outdoors/outside	kârng nôrk	ข้างนอก

over *(on top)*	bon, něuar	บน เหนือ
to overtake	sairng	แซง
to owe	Pehn nêe	เป็นหนี้
owner	jâo-kŏrng	เจ้าของ

P

package	hòr	ห่อ
packet *(cigarettes)*	sorng	ซอง
padlock	gun-jair săi-yoo	กุญแจสายยู
page	nâr	หน้า
painful	jèhp	เจ็บ
painting *(picture)*	pârp kĭan	ภาพเขียน
pair	kôo	คู่
palace	wang	วัง
paper	gra-dàrt	กระดาษ
parcel	hòr	ห่อ
parents	pôr-mâir	พ่อแม่
to park	jòrt	จอด
party	ngarn líang	งานเลี้ยง
passenger	pôo-dohy-sărn	ผู้โดยสาร
passport	năng-sěur dern-tarng	หนังสือเดินทาง
path	tarng	ทาง
patient *(hospital)*	kon kâi	คนไข้
pattern	lûat-lai	ลวดลาย
pavement	tarng táo	ทางเท้า
to pay	jài	จ่าย
peanut	tùa lí-sŏng	ถั่วลิสง
pedestrian	kon dern táo	คนเดินเท้า
to peel	Pòrk	ปอก
pen	Pàrk-gar	ปากกา

pencil	din-sŏr	ดินสอ
pencil sharpener	têe lǎo din-sŏr	ที่เหลาดินสอ
penknife	měet páp	มีดพับ
people	kon	คน
green/red pepper	prík yùak	พริกหยวก
perfume	nárm-hŏrm	น้ำหอม
perhaps	barng-tee	บางที
period (*menstrual*)	mehn	เมน
perm	dàt pŏm	ดัดผม
to permit	a-nú-yârt	อนุญาต
person	kon	คน
personal	sùan Tua	ส่วนตัว
petrol	nám-man	น้ำมัน
petrol station	Pám nám-man	ปั๊มน้ำมัน
to photocopy	tài àyk-ga-sǎrn	ถ่ายเอกสาร
to photograph	tài rôop	ถ่ายรูป
photograph	rôop tài	รูปถ่าย
photographer	châng tài rôop	ช่างถ่ายรูป
phrase book	kôo-meur sŏn-ta-nar	คู่มือสนทนา
to pick (*choose*)	lêuark	เลือก
(*flowers, etc.*)	dèht	เด็ด
pickpocket	ka-mohy lúang gra-Pǎo	ขโมยล้วงกระเป๋า
picture	rôop	รูป
piece	chín	ชิ้น
pig	mǒo	หมู
pillow	mŏrn	หมอน
pillowcase	Plòrk mŏrn	ปลอกหมอน
pin	kěhm mùt	เข็มหมุด
pipe (*smoking*)	glôrng yar-sòop	กล้องยาสูบ
(*drain*)	tôr nárm	ท่อน้ำ
place	sa-tǎrn-têe	สถานที่

plane	krêuarng bin	เครื่องบิน
plant	Tôn mái	ต้นไม้
plaster (*sticking*)	plárt-sa-Têr Pìt plàir	พลาสเตอร์ปิดแผล
plastic	plárt-sa-Tĭk	พลาสติค
plastic bag	tŭng plárt-sa-Tĭk	ถุงพลาสติค
plate	jarn	จาน
platform	charn char-lar	ชานชาลา
to play	lêhn	เล่น
please: could you please …?	chûay … ช่วย	ช่วย
pleased	por jai	พอใจ
plenty	mârk mai	มากมาย
pliers	keem	คีม
plug	Plák	ปลั๊ก
pocket	gra-Păo	กระเป๋า
to point at	chée	ชี้
poison	yar pít	ยาพิษ
poisonous	Pehn pít	เป็นพิษ
police(man)	Tam-rùat	ตำรวจ
police station	sa-tăr-nee Tam-rùat	สถานีตำรวจ
polish (*for shoes*)	yar kàt rorng-táo	ยาขัดรองเท้า
polite	sù-pârp	สุภาพ
politician	nák garn meuarng	นักการเมือง
pool (*swimming*)	sà wâi nárm	สระว่ายน้ำ
poor (*not rich*)	jon	จน
pork	néuar mŏo	เนื้อหมู
port (*quayside*)	târ reuar	ท่าเรือ
porter (*hotel*)	kon fâo Pra-Too	คนเฝ้าประตู
possible	Pehn Pai dâi	เป็นไปได้
to post	sòng jòt-măi	ส่งจดหมาย
post	jòt-măi	จดหมาย
post-box	Tôo Prai-sa-nee	ตู้ไปรษณีย์

postcard	Póht-sa-gárt	โปสการ์ด
post office	Prai-sa-nee	ไปรษณีย์
to postpone	lêuarn	เลื่อน
potato	man fa-ràng	มันฝรั่ง
to pour	tay	เท
powder	Pâirng	แป้ง
powdered milk	nom pŏng	นมผง
power (*electricity*)	fai-fár	ไฟฟ้า
power cut	fai dàp	ไฟดับ
prawn	gûng	กุ้ง
to prefer	chôrp mârk gwàr	ชอบมากกว่า
pregnant	mee tórng	มีท้อง
to prepare	Triam	เตรียม
prescription	bai sàng yar	ใบสั่งยา
pretty	sŭay	สวย
price	rar-kar	ราคา
prime minister	nar-yók	นายก
prince	jâo chai	เจ้าชาย
princess	jâo yĭng	เจ้าหญิง
prison	reuarn-jam	เรือนจำ
	kúk (*casual word*)	คุก
private	sùan Tua	ส่วนตัว
prize	rarng-wan	รางวัล
problem	Pan-hăr	ปัญหา
prohibited	hârm	ห้าม
to promise	săn-yar	สัญญา
to pronounce	òrk sĭang	ออกเสียง
prostitute	sŏh-pay-nee	โสเภณี
public	săr-tar-ra-ná	สาธารณะ
public holiday	wan yùt rârt-cha-garn	วันหยุดราชการ
to pull	deuhng	ดึง

puncture	yarng Tàirk	ยางแตก
purse	gra-Păo sa-Tarng	กระเป๋าสตางค์
to push	plàk	ผลัก
pyjamas	chút norn	ชุดนอน

Q

queen	rar-chì-nee	ราชินี
question	kam tărm	คำถาม
queue	kiw	คิว
quick	rehw	เร็ว
quiet	ngîap	เงียบ
quite: quite a lot	mârk tee diaw	มากทีเดียว

R

rabbit	gra-Tài	กระต่าย
racecourse	sa-nărm már	สนามม้า
racket (*tennis*)	ráihk-gèht	แร็กเก็ต
radiator (*car*)	môr nárm	หม้อน้ำ
radio	wít-ta-yú	วิทยุ
railway	rót fai	รถไฟ
railway station	sa-tăr-nee rót fai	สถานีรถไฟ
railway track	tarng rót fai	ทางรถไฟ
rain	fŏn	ฝน
it's raining	fŏn Tòk	ฝนตก
to rape	kòm-kĕurn	ข่มขืน
rare	hăr yârk	หายาก
rat	nŏo	หนู
raw	dìp	ดิบ
razor	mêet gohn	มีดโกน
razor blade	bai mêet gohn	ใบมีดโกน

to reach	Pai těuhng	ไปถึง
to read	àrn	อ่าน
ready	prórm	พร้อม
real (*authentic*)	kŏrng táir	ของแท้
really	jing-jing	จริง ๆ
rear	kârng lăng	ข้างหลัง
receipt	bai sèht	ใบเสร็จ
to recognize	jam dâi	จำได้
to recommend	náih-nam	แนะนำ
reduction (*price*)	lót rar-kar	ลดราคา
refrigerator	Tôo yehn	ตู้เย็น
to refund	keurn ngern	คืนเงิน
religion	sàrt-sa-năr	ศาสนา
to remember	jam dâi	จำได้
to rent	châo	เช่า
rent	kâr châo	ค่าเช่า
to repair	sôrm	ซ่อม
to reply	Tòrp	ตอบ
to reserve	jorng	จอง
restaurant	rárn ar-hărn	ร้านอาหาร
to return	glàp	กลับ
return (*ticket*)	Tŭa Pai-glàp	ตั๋วไปกลับ
reverse-charge call	gèhp ngern Plai tarng	เก็บเงินปลายทาง
ribbon	ríp-bîn	ริบบิ้น
rice	kâo	ข้าว
rice field	tûng nar	ทุ่งนา
rich	ruay	รวย
to ride	kèe	ขี่
right (*correct*)	tòok	ถูก
(*not left*)	kwăr	ขวา
right-handed	ta-nàt kwăr	ถนัดขวา

ring (*jewellery*)	wăirn	แหวน
ripe	sùk	สุก
river	mâir-nárm	แม่น้ำ
road	ta-nŏn	ถนน
to rob	Plôn	ปล้น
roof	lăng-kar	หลังคา
room (*hotel, etc.*)	hôrng	ห้อง
(*space*)	têe wârng	ที่ว่าง
rope	chêuark	เชือก
rose (*flower*)	dòrk gù-làrp	ดอกกุหลาบ
rotten	nâo	เน่า
round	glom	กลม
roundabout	wong-wian	วงเวียน
row (*n*)	tăihw	แถว
rubber (*material*)	yarng	ยาง
rubbish (*waste*)	ka-yà	ขยะ
rucksack	Pây lăng	เป้หลัง
rude	yàrp kai	หยาบคาย
ruler (*for measuring*)	mâi ban-tát	ไม้บันทัด
to run	wîng	วิ่ง

S

sad	sâo	เศร้า
safe (*strong box*)	Tôo sáyp	ตู้เซฟ
(*secure*)	Plòrt pai	ปลอดภัย
safety pin	kĕhm glàt	เข็มกลัด
salad	sa-làt	สลัด
sale	lót rar-kar	ลดราคา
same	mĕuarn gan	เหมือนกัน
sample	Tua-yàrng	ตัวอย่าง

sand	sai	ทราย
sandals	rorng-táo-Tàih	รองเท้าแตะ
sanitary towels	pâr a-nar-mai	ผ้าอนามัย
sauce	nám jĭm	น้ำจิ้ม
saucer	jarn rorng	จานรอง
sausage	sâi-gròrk	ไส้กรอก
to save (rescue)	chûay-lěuar	ช่วยเหลือ
to say	pôot	พูด
scald	plǎir lûak	แผลลวก
scarf	pâr pan kor	ผ้าพันคอ
school	rohng rian	โรงเรียน
scissors	gan-gai	กรรไกร
screwdriver	kǎi kuang	ไขควง
sculpture	rôop-pân	รูปปั้น
sea	ta-lay	ทะเล
seafood	ar-hǎrn ta-lay	อาหารทะเล
seasick	mao klêurn	เมาคลื่น
season	réuh-doo	ฤดู
seat	têe nâng	ที่นั่ง
seat-belt	kěhm-kàt ni-ra-pai	เข็มขัดนิรภัย
second (after first)	têe sǒrng	ที่สอง
(period of time)	wí-nar-tee	วินาที
secret	kwarm láp	ความลับ
secretary	lay-kǎr-nú-garn	เลขานุการ
to see (with eyes)	morng hěhn	มองเห็น
to sell	kǎi	ขาย
sellotape	sa-gót táyp	สก็อตเทป
to send	sòng	ส่ง
separately	yâirk gan	แยกกัน
serious	rái-rairng	ร้ายแรง
to serve	bor-ri-garn	บริการ

several	lăi	หลาย
shampoo	chairm-poo sà pŏm	แชมพูสระผม
shark	Plar cha-lărm	ปลาฉลาม
sharksfin soup	(súp) hŏo cha-lărm	(ซุป) หูฉลาม
sharp	kom	คม
to shave	gohn	โกน
shaving cream/foam	kreem gohn nùat	ครีมโกนหนวด
she	káo	เขา
sheet (*of paper*)	pàihn	แผ่น
(*for bed*)	pâr Poo têe-norn	ผ้าปูที่นอน
shelf	hîng	หิ้ง
ship	reuar	เรือ
shirt	sêuar chért	เสื้อเชิร์ต
shoe	rorng-táo	รองเท้า
shoelaces	chêuark pòok rorng-táo	เชือกผูกรองเท้า
shoe polish	yar kàt rorng-táo	ยาขัดรองเท้า
shop	rárn	ร้าน
shop assistant	pa-nák-ngarn kăi	พนักงานขาย
short (*length*)	sân	สั้น
(*not tall*)	Tîa	เตี้ย
shorts	garng-gayng kăr sân	กางเกงขาสั้น
to shout	Ta-gohn	ตะโกน
to show	sa-dairng	แสดง
shower	fàk-bua	ฝักบัว
to shrink	hòt	หด
to shut	Pìt	ปิด
sick (*ill*)	Pùay, mâi sa-bai (*interchangeable*)	ป่วย ไม่สบาย
to be sick	ar-jian	อาเจียร
side	kârng	ข้าง
to sign	long chêur	ลงชื่อ

	sehn *(casual word)*	เช่น
sign	krêuarng măi	เครื่องหมาย
signal	săn-yarn	สัญญาณ
signature	lai sehn	ลายเซ็น
silent	ngîap	เงียบ
silk	pâr măi	ผ้าไหม
silver	ngern	เงิน
similar	mĕuarn gan	เหมือนกัน
simple	ngâi	ง่าย
since	Tâng-Tàir nán	ตั้งแต่นั้น
to sing	rórng playng	ร้องเพลง
single *(room)*	hôrng điaw	ห้องเดียว
(ticket)	Tŭa tîaw-diaw	ตั๋วเที่ยวเดียว
(unmarried)	Pehn sòht	เป็นโสด
to sink	jom	จม
sister *(older)*	pêe săo	พี่สาว
(younger)	nórng săo	น้องสาว
sister-in-law *(older)*	pêe sa-pái	พี่สะใภ้
(younger)	nórng sa-pái	น้องสะใภ้
to sit	nâng	นั่ง
size	ka-nàrt	ขนาด
skin	năng	หนัง
skirt	gra-Prohng	กระโปรง
sky	tórng-fár	ท้องฟ้า
to sleep	norn làp	นอนหลับ
sleeper/sleeping-car	rót norn	รถนอน
sleeve	kăirn sêuar	แขนเสื้อ
slice	chín	ชิ้น
slide *(film)*	sa-lái	สไลด์
slim	pŏrm	ผอม
to slip	lêurn	ลื่น

slow	chár	ช้า
small	léhk	เล็ก
to smell	dâi glìn	ได้กลิ่น
to smile	yím	ยิ้ม
to smoke	sòop bu-rèe	สูบบุหรี่
smoke	kwan	ควัน
smooth	rîap	เรียบ
snake	ngoo	งู
to sneeze	jarm	จาม
so (thus)	dang nán	ดังนั้น
soap	sa-bòo	สบู่
sock	tŭng táo	ถุงเท้า
soda water	nárm soh-dar	น้ำโซดา
soft	nîm	นิ่ม
soldier	ta-hărn	ทหาร
sold out	kăi mòt láirw	ขายหมดแล้ว
sole (shoe)	péurn rorng-táo	พื้นรองเท้า
somebody	barng kon	บางคน
something	barng an	บางอัน
sometimes	barng tee	บางที
somewhere	barng têe	บางที่
son	lôok chai	ลูกชาย
song	playng	เพลง
son-in-law	lôok kŏei	ลูกเขย
soon	mâi chár	ไม่ช้า
sore	jèhp	เจ็บ
sorry	kŏr-tôht	ขอโทษ
sound (voice)	sĭang	เสียง
soup	súp	ซุป
sour	Prîaw	เปรี้ยว
south	tít Tâi	ทิศใต้

souvenir	kŏrng têe ra-léuhk	ของที่ระลึก
spanner	gun-jair Pàrk Tai	กุญแจปากตาย
spare parts	a-lài	อะหลั่ย
spare tyre	yarng a-lài	ยางอะหลั่ย
to speak	pôot	พูด
special	pí-sàyt	พิเศษ
spectacles	wâihn-Tar	แว่นตา
speed	kwarm rehw	ความเร็ว
to spend *(money)*	chái jài	ใช้จ่าย
spider	mairng mum	แมงมุม
spoon	chórn	ช้อน
sport	gee-lar	กีฬา
sprained	plairng, kléht *(interchangeable)*	แพลง เคล็ด
stain	roy, krârp *(interchangeable)*	รอย คราบ
stairs	ban-dai	บันได
stamp *(postage)*	sa-Tairm	แสตมป์
to stand	yeurn	ยืน
star	dao	ดาว
to start	rêrm	เริ่ม
station	sa-tăr-nee	สถานี
to steal	ka-mohy	ขโมย
step *(of stairs)*	kân ban-dai	ขั้นบันได
steward *(air)*	sa-júat	สจ๊วร์ต
stewardess *(air)*	air hóht-tàyt	แอร์โฮสเตส
sticky rice	kâo nĭaw	ข้าวเหนียว
stockings	tŭng nôrng	ถุงน่อง
stolen	tòok ka-mohy	ถูกขโมย
stone	hĭn	หิน
to stop	jòrt, yùt *(interchangeable)*	จอด หยุด

storm	par-yú	พายุ
straight	Trong	ตรง
stranger	kon Plàirk nâr	คนแปลกหน้า
straw (*drinking*)	lòrt	หลอด
stream	lam-tarn	ลำธาร
street	ta-nŏn	ถนน
side street	soy	ซอย
string	chêuark	เชือก
striped	lai	ลาย
strong	kăihng-rairng	แข็งแรง
student	nák sèuhk-săr	นักศึกษา
to study	rian năng-sĕur	เรียนหนังสือ
suit	sòot	สูท
suitcase	gra-Păo dern-tarng	กระเป๋าเดินทาง
sun	prá-ar-tít	พระอาทิตย์
to sunbathe	àrp-dàirt	อาบแดด
sunburnt	tòok dàirt păo	ถูกแดดเผา
sunglasses	wâihn gan dàirt	แว่นกันแดด
sunshade	rôm gan dàirt	ร่มกันแดด
sunstroke	Pehn lom dàirt	เป็นลมแดด
sure	nâir-jai	แน่ใจ
surname	narm sa-gun	นามสกุล
to sweat	ngèuar òrk	เหงื่อออก
sweat	ngèuar	เหงื่อ
sweet (*taste*)	wărn	หวาน
sweet and sour	Prîaw-wărn	เปรี้ยวหวาน
to swim	wâi nárm	ว่ายน้ำ
swimming pool	sà wâi nárm	สระว่ายน้ำ
to switch off (*lights, etc.*)	Pìt	ปิด
to switch on (*lights, etc.*)	Pèrt	เปิด
swollen	buam	บวม

| symptom | ar-garn | อาการ |
| system | ra-bòp | ระบบ |

T

table	Tó	โต๊ะ
to take	ao Pai	เอาไป
to take off (*clothes, etc.*)	tòrt	ถอด
talcum powder	Pâirng	แป้ง
to talk	pôot	พูด
tall	sŏong	สูง
tame	chêuarng	เชื่อง
tap	gók nárm	ก๊อกน้ำ
tape	táyp	เทป
tape measure	săi wát	สายวัด
to taste	chim	ชิม
taste	rót	รส
taxi	táihk-sêe	แท็กซี่
tea	char	ชา
tea bag	char tŭng	ชาถุง
to teach	sŏrn	สอน
teacher	kroo	ครู
to tear	chèek	ฉีก
teaspoon	chórn char	ช้อนชา
teenager	wai rûn	วัยรุ่น
telegram	toh-ra-lâyk	โทรเลข
telephone	toh-ra-sàp	โทรศัพท์
television	toh-ra-tát	โทรทัศน์
telex	tay-lèhk	เทเล็กส์
to tell	bòrk	บอก
temperature	un-ha-poom	อุณหภูมิ

to have a temperature	Pehn kâi	เป็นไข้
temple (*religious*)	wát	วัด
temporary	chûa-krao	ชั่วคราว
tent	Tén	เต็นท์
terrible	yâir mârk	แย่มาก
than	gwàr	กว่า
thank you	kòrp kun	ขอบคุณ
that (*person*)	kon nán	คนนั้น
(*things*)	an nán	อันนั้น
theatre	rohng-la-korn	โรงละคร
their/theirs	kŏrng káo	ของเขา
them	káo	เขา
then	Torn nán	ตอนนั้น
there	têe nân	ที่นั้น
therefore	dang nán	ดังนั้น
thermometer	Pa-ròrt	ปรอท
these	pûak née	พวกนี้
they (*people*)	káo	เขา
(*things*)	man	มัน
thick	nǎr	หนา
thief	ka-mohy	ขโมย
thin	barng	บาง
thing	sìng-kŏrng	สิ่งของ
to think	kít	คิด
third	têe sǎrm	ที่สาม
thirsty	hǐw nárm	หิวน้ำ
this (*person*)	kon née	คนนี้
(*things*)	an née	อันนี้
those	pûak nán	พวกนั้น
thread	dâi	ด้าย
through	pàrn	ผ่าน

to throw	kwârng	ขว้าง
to throw away	tíng	ทิ้ง
thunder	fár rórng	ฟ้าร้อง
thunderstorm	par-yú fŏn	พายุฝน
ticket	Tŭa	ตั๋ว
ticket office	hôrng kăi Tŭa	ห้องขายตั๋ว
tide	gra-săir nárm	กระแสน้ำ
to tie	pòok	ผูก
tie	néhk-tai	เน็คไท
tight	káp	คับ
tights	tŭng-nôrng	ถุงน่อง
time	way-lar	เวลา
timetable	Tar-rarng way-lar	ตารางเวลา
tin (can)	gra-Pŏrng	กระป๋อง
tin-opener	têe Pèrt gra-Pŏrng	ที่เปิดกระป๋อง
tip (money)	típ	ทิป
tired	nèuary	เหนื่อย
tissues	gra-dàrt chéht meur	กระดาษเช็ดมือ
to (arrive)	Pai tĕuhng	ไปถึง
toast (bread)	ka-nŏm-Pang Pîng	ขนมปังปิ้ง
tobacco	yar sòop	ยาสูบ
today	wan née	วันนี้
together	dûay gan	ด้วยกัน
toilet	hôrng nárm	ห้องน้ำ
toilet paper	gra-dàrt cham-rá	กระดาษชำระ
tomato	ma-kĕuar-tâyt	มะเขือเทศ
tomorrow	prûng-née	พรุ่งนี้
tonight	keurn née	คืนนี้
too (excessive)	gern Pai	เกินไป
(as well)	dûay	ด้วย
tool	krêuarng meur	เครื่องมือ

toothbrush	Prairng sĕe fan	แปรงสีฟัน
toothpaste	yar sĕe fan	ยาสีฟัน
toothpick	mái jîm fan	ไม้จิ้มฟัน
top	yôrt	ยอด
torch	fai chăi	ไฟฉาย
torn	kàrt	ขาด
total	táng-mòt	ทั้งหมด
to touch	Tàih	แตะ
tourist	nák tôrng-tîaw	นักท่องเที่ยว
tourist office	săm-nák-ngarn garn tôrng-tîaw	สำนักงานการท่องเที่ยว
to tow	lârk	ลาก
towel	pâr chét Tua	ผ้าเช็ดตัว
town	meuarng	เมือง
town centre	jai glarng meuarng	ใจกลางเมือง
toy	kŏrng lâyn	ของเล่น
traffic jam	rót Tìt	รถติด
traffic lights	săn-yarn fai	สัญญาณไฟ
train	rót fai	รถไฟ
trainers	rorng-táo gee-lar	รองเท้ากีฬา
to translate	Plair	แปล
translation	kam Plair	คำแปล
travel agent	tra-wêrn ay-yâyn	ทราเวิลเอเย่นต์
traveller's cheques	chéhk dern tarng	เช็คเดินทาง
tray	tàrt	ถาด
treatment	rák-săr	รักษา
tree	Tôn mái	ต้นไม้
trousers	garng-gayng	กางเกง
truck	rót ban-túk	รถบรรทุก
true	jing	จริง
to try (test)	lorng	ลอง

to type	pim dèet	พิมพ์ดีด
typewriter	krêuarng pim dèet	เครื่องพิมพ์ดีด
tyre	yarng rót	ยางรถ

U

ugly	kêe-rày	ขี้เหร่
umbrella	rôm	ร่ม
uncle (*older brother of father or mother*)	lung	ลุง
(*younger brother of father*) ar		อา
(*younger brother of mother*) nár		น้า
uncomfortable	mâi sa-bai	ไม่สบาย
under(neath)	Tâi	ใต้
to understand	kâo-jai	เข้าใจ
I don't understand	mâi kâo-jai	ไม่เข้าใจ
underwater	Tâi nárm	ใต้น้ำ
underwear	garng-gayng nai	กางเกงใน
to undress	tòrt sêuar	ถอดเสื้อ
uniform (*n*)	krêuarng-bàirp	เครื่องแบบ
university	ma-hăr wít-ta-yar-lai	มหาวิทยาลัย
unless	wáyn Tàir	เว้นแต่
until	jon gwàr	จนกว่า
unwell	mâi sa-bai	ไม่สบาย
up	kêuhn Pai	ขึ้นไป
upper	kârng bon	ข้างบน
upstairs	chán bon	ชั้นบน
urgent	dùan	ด่วน
us	rao	เรา
to use	chái	ใช้

V

vacant	wârng	ว่าง
valuables	kŏrng mee kâr	ของมีค่า
van	rót Tôo	รถตู้
vase	jair-gan	แจกัน
VAT	par-sĕe moon-kâr pêrm	ภาษีมูลค่าเพิ่ม
	wáiht *(casual word)*	แว็ต
vegetables	pàk	ผัก
vegetarian	mâi gin néuar	ไม่กินเนื้อ
very	mârk	มาก
vet	sàt-Ta-wá-pâirt	สัตวแพทย์
video camera	glôrng wee-dee-oh	กล้องวิดีโอ
video cassette	táyp wee-dee-oh	เทปวิดีโอ
view	tiw-tát	ทิวทัศน์
village	mòo-bârn	หมู่บ้าน
visa	wee-sâr	วีซ่า
to visit *(holidays)*	Pai tîaw	ไปเที่ยว
(social call)	Pai yîam	ไปเยี่ยม
vitamin	wí-Tar-min	วิตามิน
voice	sĭang	เสียง

W

to wait	ror	รอ
waiter/waitress	kon sèrp	คนเสิร์ฟ
to walk	dern	เดิน
walking stick	mái táo	ไม้เท้า
wall *(inside)*	făr pa-năng	ฝาผนัง
(outside)	gam-pairng	กำแพง
wallet	gra-Păo sa-Tarng	กระเป๋าสตางค์
to want	Tôrng-garn	ต้องการ

warm	òp-ùn	อบอุ่น
to wash	lárng	ล้าง
washing powder	pǒng sák fôrk	ผงซักฟอก
to watch	fâo doo	เฝ้าดู
watch	nar-lí-gar kôr meur	นาฬิกาข้อมือ
water	nárm	น้ำ
waterfall	nárm-Tòk	น้ำตก
waterproof	gan nárm	กันน้ำ
wave (sea)	klêurn	คลื่น
wax: sealing wax	krâng	ครั่ง
way (route)	tarng	ทาง
we	rao	เรา
weather	ar-gàrt	อากาศ
wedding	pí-tee Tàirng-ngarn	พิธีแต่งงาน
week	sàp-dar	สัปดาห์
weekly	rai sàp-dar	รายสัปดาห์
to weigh	châng nám-nàk	ชั่งน้ำหนัก
weight	nám-nàk	น้ำหนัก
well (adv)	dee	ดี
west	tít Ta-wan-Tòk	ทิศตะวันตก
wet	Pìak	เปียก
what	a-rai	อะไร
wheel	lór	ล้อ
steering wheel	puang mar-lai	พวงมาลัย
wheelchair	rót kěhn	รถเข็น
when	mêuar-rài	เมื่อไหร่
where	têe năi	ที่ไหน
which	an năi	อันไหน
while	ka-nà-têe	ขณะที่
who	krai	ใคร
whole	táng-mòt	ทั้งหมด

why	tam-mai	ทำไม
wide	gwârng	กว้าง
widow	mâir mâi	แม่ม่าย
widower	pôr mâi	พ่อม่าย
wife	pan-ra-yar	ภรรยา
	mia (casual word)	เมีย
to win	cha-ná	ชนะ
wind	lom	ลม
window	nâr-Tàrng	หน้าต่าง
to windsurf	win-sérp	วินเซิร์ฟ
windy	lom rairng	ลมแรง
wing	Pèek	ปีก
with	gàp	กับ
without	mâi mee, mâi ao	ไม่มี ไม่เอา
woman	pôo-yĭng	ผู้หญิง
wood (material)	mái	ไม้
wool	kŏn sàt	ขนสัตว์
word	kam	คำ
to work	tam-ngarn	ทำงาน
It doesn't work	mâi tam-ngarn	ไม่ทำงาน
world	lôhk	โลก
worm	nŏrn	หนอน
worried	wí-Tòk	วิตก
wound (injury)	bàrt-plăir	บาดแผล
to wrap	hòr	ห่อ
to write	kĭan	เขียน
writing paper	gra-dàrt kĭan năng-sĕur	กระดาษเขียนหนังสือ
wrong	pìt	ผิด

X

| X-ray | éhk-sa-ray | เอ็กซ์เรย์ |

Y

to yawn	hăo	หาว
year	Pee	ปี
yes	châi	ใช่
yesterday	mêuar warn née	เมื่อวานนี้
yet	yang	ยัง
you	kun	คุณ
young (*man*)	nùm	หนุ่ม
(*woman*)	săo	สาว
(*child*)	dèhk	เด็ก
your/yours	kŏrng kun	ของคุณ
youth	nùm săo	หนุ่มสาว

Z

| zip | síp | ซิป |
| zoo | sŭan sàt | สวนสัตว์ |

Dictionary

BBC Books publishes courses on the following languages:

ARABIC	ITALIAN
CHINESE	JAPANESE
FRENCH	PORTUGUESE
GERMAN	RUSSIAN
GREEK	SPANISH
HINDI & URDU	TURKISH

Developed by BBC Language Unit
Cover designed by Peter Bridgewater and Annie Moss
Project Manager: Stenton Associates
Design: Steve Pitcher
Series Editor: Carol Stanley

Published by BBC Books
A division of BBC Worldwide Ltd
Woodlands, 80 Wood Lane, London W12 OTT

ISBN 0563 39912 0

First published 1995

Text and Cover printed in Great Britain by Clays Ltd,
St Ives Plc